Rolling with the Punches
My Persevering Battle with Multiple Sclerosis
by:
Louise Huey Greenleaf

Believe in you!
Louise

Rolling with the Punches-
My Persevering Battle with
Multiple Sclerosis
by Louise Huey Greenleaf
Copyright ©2017
All Rights Reserved

This book may not be reproduced in whole or in part for any reason without prior written consent from the author.
All Scripture quotations, unless otherwise indicated, are taken from the Holy Bible, New International Version®, NIV®. Copyright ©1973, 1978, 1984, 2011 by Biblica, Inc.™ Used by permission of Zondervan. All rights reserved worldwide. www.zondervan.com The "NIV" and "New International Version" are trademarks registered in the United States Patent and Trademark Office by Biblica, Inc.™

Cover Photo courtesy of:
Barbara Thompson

Published by:
Proper Publishing
theproperpublisher@yahoo.com
Interior and cover design ©2017
by Proper Publishing LLC.

Interior Images obtained
via Creative Commons:
Vintage Wildflowers
Wheelchair on road
Plywood through Telephone pole

First Printing
September 2017

Acknowledgments:

I first offer my deepest gratitude to my Three in One;

God, my creator, who has and will continue to always love me just this beautiful way He meant for me to be yesterday, today, and for eternity.

Jesus Christ, my Savior, who is the solid rock that carried my heavy burdens, and sustained my strength the countless times I really wanted to give up and crumble.

And, the Holy Spirit, who guides my EVERY turn of the wheel.
God MUST be first. For NOBODY can be anything without Him. Surely not I.

Thank you, to my devoted Publisher, Susan A. Lewis, for your unwavering, strong-willed, tough love commitment in keeping me focused on bringing Part One of this book to fruition, and promising the same to complete it with Part Two close behind. I thank you too, Susan, for believing in me through your professional coaching and encouragement to have the faith in myself so that my words may help others who go through the same or similar experiences I and my family have gone through for almost four decades.

I give my heartfelt thanks to my beautiful friend, Emily McElfresh, for editing and correcting my over-abundant, atrocious punctuation errors, and helping me to separate long running sentences with the correct markings set in their proper places in order to make sense for the reader. (and me!)

I am especially grateful to Shanda Trofe, my Publisher and Founder of Spiritual Writers Network, CEO of Transcendent Publishing. Shanda is the angel who made my dream come true as a published author, by selecting a number of my stories and poems to be included in seven of the network's contest books since 2013. But, mainly for her excellence in coaching aspiring writers like myself, to take the proper steps in the writing and publishing process, in her genuine loving way. Thank you for taking me under your wings and teaching me to fly through my thoughts and words.

- Touched by an Angel ~ A Collection of Divinely Inspired Stories and Poems / Titanium Angel ~ My Journey with Multiple Sclerosis

- Whispers of the Soul ~ A Poetry Anthology / SUCCUMP-TION-ACITY (3rd Place Winner)

- The Best of Spiritual Writers Network 2014 / A Precious Memory

- Illuminations of the Soul ~ A Poetry Anthology / Millions of Reasons to Smile Today

- Finding Our Wings ~ A Collection of Angelic Stories and Poems / Angels Watching Over Me (Title by Krista Gawronski; Subtitle by Louise Huey Greenleaf

- The Peacemakers ~ Restoring Love in the World through Stories of Compassion and Wisdom / Forward by Louise Huey Greenleaf

- The Best of Spiritual Writers Network 2016 / The Hands of Love (1st Place Winner)

Thank you, with all my heart to Author, Inspirational Speaker, Publisher and Founder of the DreamStrong Foundation, as well as CEO for OptiMystic Press Publishing, Connie Gorrell and world-renowned author, inspirational speaker, spiritual teacher and psychic medium, Sunny Dawn Johnston, for including my chapter in our beautiful, inspiring book,

- The Invisible Thread ~ True Stories of Synchronicity with Sunny Dawn Johnston and Friends / Silky Tales of Eternal Grace

- The Gift of Inspiration for Women / Fly Away and Dance & Millions of Reasons to Smile Today.

A HUGE thank you to ALL my talented brothers and sisters of the written word. You inspire me so with your God given abilities to move the emotions of people around the world, including me. Through the words you choose to create and publish such awesome stories, articles, blogs, poems…et cetera…you have taught me that it is A ok to have the courage to share my own thoughts.

To my over the top, talented photographer, Barbara Thompson. God truly blessed you with the keen ability to capture beauty even in that which most cannot see or even are repulsed by. Thank you for taking part in making my cover photo to this book so exquisitely attractive.

Thank you, is such a minuscule word when it comes to expressing gratitude to my superhero husband, Don. You have LITTERALLY carried me through our journey together as husband and wife for almost forty years. If not for you, I would have stopped being many years ago. There is NO ONE on this earth who could take the utmost loving care of me that you have with such deep love, devotion, understanding and strength. Though the journey has been tough pretty much right from the very start, our impassioned love for one another has prevailed above EVERY obstacle that we have been faced with. I love you more than love. I cherish you! Always and forever!

I am so very grateful to my precious daughter, Krissy, for her over the top love and encouragement in getting this book published. Thank you for introducing me to Susan, who is not only my publisher, but my beautiful friend as well. There are no words to say how much I love you, my sweet daughter. For there is NOT ONE on this earth who loves you more than me, and I look forward to reading your chapter in Part Two.

To ALL of my caring, loving friends, thank you, for always taking interest in my writing endeavors since I started publishing some of my stories and poems since 2013. I am grateful that you are anticipating the publishing of this book that you have heard about for so long. Part One is FINALLY in your hands, and I pray you will enjoy it and look forward to reading about my journey with multiple sclerosis in Part Two…soon to follow.

DEDICATION:

I dedicate this book to my beautiful husband, Don. For this is OUR story, and you are my EVERYTHING! I will love you for eternity.

To my sweet daughter, Krissy, you are, quite simply, the GREATEST love of my life!

This book is compassionately dedication to ALL who bravely live with chronic illness throughout the world.

"*It* is no mistake that to suffer means to feel keenly. For to feel deeply and precisely with full awareness is what opens us to both joy and sorrow. It is the capacity to feel keenly that reveals the meaning of our experiences."
~Mark Nepo

Part One
Training Wheels

SUCCUMP-TION-ACITY

My limbs grow tired,
invisible weights upon my feet
struggling to appear as before.
Hesitant actions in response to my thoughts.
The muscles straining,
making movements a chore.
I knew this might happen,
a fear kept deep down inside.
My thoughts overwhelm me.
I just want to hide my frailties and weaknesses,
my need to have a cry.
Will I be the same again?
I must continue to try!
Talk to God, he'll listen.
Close your eyes and pray.
When one road is blocked,
another surely *will* open your way.
Perhaps it's time to set the high heels and cute shoes aside,
and instead sing of God's glory in joy and in pride.
For it *is* more than just *one* gift that I have from Heaven above.
Oh yes, I have *so many* gifts to share
in the light of His *never* ending love.

Preface

Multiple sclerosis is such a mean disease! I know firsthand because I have fiercely battled it for almost 38 years now as it maliciously and continuously punctures the deepest of my core. It stalks me day and night – no matter where I am, and cynically aims to steal no less than everything I am physically and emotionally. It has interfered with fulfilling hopes and dreams I have strived to accomplish, and unabatingly attempts to sabotage relationships with those to whom I am closest with. It is sneaky and strikes its victims without warning, without exemption – with NO mercy!

I have written this book to tell MY story, MY truth, in MY own words about the way things REALLY are living with multiple sclerosis, a chronic, incurable, and progressive disease that has confined me to a wheelchair for the rest of my life. I am releasing thirty-eight years of bottled up STUFF – the bad, and the wonderful. I'm telling it the way I need to – the way I TRULY feel. Yes, I am FINALLY giving my soul permission to let it ALL out, and I am holding NOTHING back, nor am I sugarcoating my unthinkable journey in ways where people will view me as some heroin of strength and courage, because I am NOT that. I am merely a person who wishes to free my soul as I acknowledge my losses, while more importantly realizing the amazing blessings that I have so richly acquired through God with sincere gratitude for ALL that I have, and ALL who I am – despite the horrendous affects multiple sclerosis has cruelly imposed upon not only my life, but my loved one's as well.

Through the years, I have documented many of my accounts for no one more than me, myself, and I, with the absolute reality that no one wishes to constantly hear me spill the unbecoming burdens that I have been forced to deal with every single day of my adult life – which is going on thirty-eight of my fifty-eight years. And though it has been an awesome journey in many more ways than all that multiple sclerosis has unkindly denuded from me, and held me back from living my life at the pace I should be able to for the age I am, and how easy I make it look way too much of the time, I can surely attest in saying that there is not ONE human being on this planet who wouldn't cry, complain, cuss like a foul-mouthed sailor, scream at the top of their lungs, roll over everything in the way, and ask God – WHY ME? WHY ANYONE? But then again…WHY NOT? I would certainly rather it be me than ANY OTHER!

So I promised myself that I will *always* be right here to listen to *me* – both my highs and lows, with compassion and love. Yes, I am just saying it like it is, and I am not holding back on ANYTHING! I need to do this. I need to be able to relieve myself, and hopefully encourage others to share their stories as well, because frankly, in more ways than not – even though I have been incredibly blessed to be so loved and supported by my selfless, devoted husband of thirty-eight years... Don, who has ALWAYS been here for me. Still, I feel so disconnected, isolated, and excluded redundantly more than just on occasion. So I will begin sharing my adventures with a quirky poem I wrote that always makes me laugh, and helps to lighten my frequent bouts of sadness and frustration. Hey, let's face it, in the long run we are ALL, each and every one of us – *alone*. But despite the many losses I and many others have had no choice other than to endure and suffer through, I would not trade *even a moment* for all that I have been blessed to so richly have acquired through God's loving grace and ceaseless presence.

I have fought back HARD right from the start, and I will NOT surrender! So help me God, I WILL endure until the day comes when I take my last earthly breath and return to the eternal universal light. I WILL stay true to my faith with absolute knowledge that God's presence has and ALWAYS will be with me to give me the strength and courage it takes to persevere and keep ROLLING WITH THE PUNCHES!

Let my journey be told!

Chronicles of an Invalid

I have multiple sclerosis and osteoporosis,
a sty in my left eye,
how come all I do is cry?
Lymphedema, spasms,
Don't DARE mess with my orgasms!

A prescription for some Actonel,
a brand-new tube of Metro Gel,
I can't walk and I can't drive,
but look at me – I'm alive!

They tell me that I'm hell on wheels,
and slippers are my new high heels.
Diapers are my new endeavor,
thongs, cute panties – GONE FOREVER!

Well, now that all is said and done
there's one thing left to say.
Whatever it is or what will be,
my hubby loves me anyway!

Chapter 1

We've only just begun

> *"So much of life ahead*
> *We'll find a place where there's room to grow*
> *and yes, we've just begun."*
> ~ Paul Williams & Roger Nichols

MARCH 1979

What a strange sort of whirling sensation I had been feeling in my head that came out of nowhere. All week long, I had been experiencing a slight inner circular movement that I had never felt before, nor could I describe the feeling other than that it was *not* even at all like that same intense dizziness we intentionally brought on ourselves as whimsical, carefree children after spinning around, and around, and around, and then suddenly stopping and clumsily stumbling off balance, trying not to fall as we waited for our equilibrium to return back to its normal state where we were again stable and sure of our grounding. No, this felt like my brain was detached from my skull – floating around freely like an unanchored boat drifting on a slightly, yet noticeable wavy sea. Oh, how in our innocent childish ignorance we did not yet understand the concept of, *"be careful what you wish for!"*

It was already Sunday afternoon. Back to work tomorrow and the heavy rain hadn't let up all weekend. But I couldn't wait any longer to get the weeks overflowing basket of dirty laundry done. I had plenty of clean clothing to get by, but Don needed his work uniforms, and we needed fresh clean towels. It would have all been done if the weather had cleared up some, or better yet, if we had the room for a washer and dryer in our small apartment. But with the constant down pouring of rain all weekend, I chose to procrastinate until the last minute to make my way down the outside stairway from our second-story apartment, to the community laundry room. As I was about halfway down the wet steps in the pouring rain, I became dizzy to the point where I was forced to stop and set the basket down as the rain soaked my body along with the clothes. After taking a moment to regroup, I finally arrived at the laundry room. Then, after resting for a few minutes, I was feeling back to normal and went on to complete the task. *"I must have some sort of virus coming on,"* I thought to myself. *"It had pestered me on and off all week! I'm sure it will pass soon."*

When Don returned home from watching the races at his buddy's place, I mentioned what had happened on my way to the laundry room, as well as the strange feelings that had been coming and going throughout the week. We both figured that I was either coming down with something, or I became overly excited and emotional when he surprised me with a diamond ring and asked me to marry him last weekend. It must have been the latter because those feelings disappeared as quickly as they appeared. So I simply put our clean laundry away, and we enjoyed the remaining hours of the weekend snuggled up on the couch watching television together. This was just the beginning of our journey. Never in our wildest thoughts did it ever cross our minds that it was really the start of decades that would be spent as not only husband and wife, but also as a dedicated caregiver and ailing spouse.

"For better or for worse. In my sickness, and in his health – until death do us part."

The LORD God said, "It is not good for the man to be alone. I will make a helper suitable for him."
~ Genesis 2:18

Chapter 2

The first time, ever I saw your face...

*"And I knew our joy would fill the earth
and last till the end of time, my love."*
~ Ewan MacColl, Peggy Seeger

Grace exists in every moment. Though we each come into this world with our own cross to carry, so, too, do we hold on to one another with fine threads that are invisible except when recognized through our hearts. When light shines upon them at just the perfect angle, they reveal a magnificent masterpiece created by one single entity whose purpose is to knit, to twist and turn, to weave and braid, to loop and plait, to construct and create into webs. These ties, perhaps metaphorically speaking, represent multitudes of incalculable stories that, even though individual, somehow intertwine and unify us somewhere along the sphere of time and throughout the Universe, urging us to meet one another, and another, and yet another. In a second of time, our souls connect to synchronize into one glorious, no longer mysterious, dimension of eternity where time will no longer be counted. Our tales will resonate to inspire God and the Universe as they are all joined together to reveal the long-awaited, all-inclusive, omnipresent, all embracing, perfectly quilted blanket of love that covers every space imaginable…even far beyond infinity.

Have you ever intentionally taken the opportunity to stop and observe a spider intricately spin its web? It is amazing how it instinctively and rhythmically places each delicate strand of silk in precise order as it continues to work without hesitation, or even the need to rest before its delicate latticework is flawlessly complete. The strands are threads of strength produced by a liquid secreted from the spiders own body and are stronger than any human being has yet been able to re-create in a material substance. Ah, except when they grow from within our hearts!

I boast to proclaim that every link within my heart represents a meaningful relationship with each possessing its own name. It would make perfect sense that those closest to the center are the ties with long-term family and friends who have been part of my life, either in its entirety or for a duration of many years. When I look at spider webs, I view them as images of our journeys – yours as well as mine, and the innumerable bonds we build along the way. Who will we meet? What motivates our desires to connect, and how will our stories unfold?

For me, it could seem as though life was destined to be a constant rigorous uphill battle, even before I was born. My parents were still teenagers and already had a two-year-old son when I arrived. The ingredients for my "welcome to the world birthday celebration" were prepared and in place… ready to serve me with a hefty portion of a deflated pink, double layered conglomeration of chaos, topped with plenty of stress and drama right from the start. But instinctively, like the spider, I immediately began my quest to build a strong and sturdy structure where I could learn to live well. It was through this web that I could survive the forces of damaging mistakes and choices made by those simply trying to do what they thought was best for me, without intending to do harm, yet in truth, they had set my journey on a topsy-turvy path of misguided direction. Hey, sometimes life isn't fair, and we get caught up in traps from which freedom seems impossible. But, somehow, through faith, courage, and persistence, we precociously march forward into battle and withstand the tests of time, meeting head on all undesired and unwelcome forces.

Though I cherish each and every relationship in my life, all unique and special in their own way, and as I consider each to be a blessing of monumental value, I must confess that there are a handful that have fully awakened my intuitive senses to the reality that they are part of a master plan that is also my destiny. I believe most would agree that some relationships are nothing short of mysteries and miracles as to how they could have possibly come to be. Perhaps, they are invisible threads perfectly placed by God's very own breath on us. I first, always with my deepest respect, offer gratitude to my maternal teachers for the parts they played in assisting God to set the wheel of my life in motion, allowing that his strategy to bring me to this earth would be carried out in order that His glory be revealed — not mine, but through me.

I give thanks to my mother who brought me into this world and gave me life. Although we were not particularly close in ways I had witnessed most mothers and daughters to normally be, and in the ways I wished and yearned for ours to be, she did the best she could with the scant degree of skills she had as a teenage mother. She would bear another two sons by the time she was twenty-one. When she and my biological father were both twenty-two years old with an infant and three other children under the age of six, myself included, they split up and divorced due to his alcoholism. He, then, fled the state, and she was left to figure out how to raise us on her own. It was a tough situation, but she loved her four children, and she did her best, despite the constant obstacles she faced daily. She then found love again when I was six years old and became pregnant with my fourth brother. They married during her pregnancy, and we became a family of seven. That is another story to be told perhaps at another time.

Though mom's age and circumstances opened questions concerning her level of wisdom to some, I know for certain a whispered thread gently blew in from God and was invisibly placed in her psyche to teach me one of my most valuable life lessons. She taught me to keep reaching for my dreams regardless of the hard work it would take to acquire that which might seem impossible. "Just always stay focused on the prize, Lou Lou, and it will come. "Jesus says in Luke 11:9 in the holy Bible: "I tell you, ask and it will be given to you; seek, and you will find; knock and the door will be opened to you."

I will always believe it was at that very moment she so perfectly wove this strand of God's wisdom into her afghan of maternal love for me, which was then marked with her very own seal of wisdom forever. It wasn't that she lacked the want or desire to give me more; she was a beautiful person who loved God and relied on her Angels. It's just that life's circumstances became too overwhelming for such a young woman to juggle. Even still, she grabbed her prize to set on her mantle of eternal history by teaching me a most valuable lesson. Makes me happy for her and for me. Thank you, Mama! Thank you, God!

Thanks, also, to my Gramma Lucy, and her sister – my auntie Sue, who surrounded me with their wings of love from the day I was born until the day Gramma died in 1984, and Auntie Sue passed in 2017. They directed me toward finding my faith in God and taught me the essential skills I needed to have in order to take care of myself, and one day to take care of a spouse and family. I will love them both always, and I miss each one immensely! Thank you, Gramma! Thank you, Auntie Sue! Thank you, God!

Not a day goes by I don't give thanks to my childhood friend, Priscilla, to whom I was attached at the hip, along with our friend, Cathy. They were best friends who grew up across the street from each other in our tiny country town in Connecticut. We were three girls brought together by way of the cheerleading squad in junior high school. They were a year ahead of me, but that didn't stop us from becoming friends and staying close to one another as we clambered our way through adolescence, facing together the dramatic dilemmas teenage girls get themselves all tied up in knots over. We were inseparable from junior high to high school and into adulthood.

When they graduated, I thought my life was over! Cathy, thankfully, stayed in the neighborhood but was busy during the day furthering her education at a nearby school. We continued to see each other, mostly on the weekends as I was still in high school. Priscilla went on to college in Miami, Florida — 1600 Long miles away. It was hard to stay in touch with her being so far, as cell phones and the internet were not yet invented; but, when she came home for holidays and breaks, we would get together and carry on as if she had never left at all.

Pris had been gone for an entire year and was rightfully enjoying her independence as a young adult with new friends, as well as spending time with a guy whom she had met and fallen in love. Cathy was involved with the fellow she would one day marry and I was working at a dinky diner in order to support myself, while at the same time auditioning for singing jobs around my home state in hopes of pursuing my dream of becoming a Broadway singing star. When I landed a part at a small theater on Long Island, New York, I thought my time had finally come; that I could break free from the dysfunctional chaotic life I had endured as a child. But really, how would I pull this off? I had no skills other than the ability to sing, had very little money, and owned an old jalopy car that barely ran. Who did I think I was other than a little girl with nothing who would probably end up always having even a lot more of nothing? My confidence and self-esteem levels were so pitifully low. God, please help me! I should know better, that to you my self-worth is so much more than I had ever imagined!

In the winter of 1978, Pris called, giddy and ecstatic with the news: Her guy had proposed marriage! Though I would not be a member of the wedding party, which would be taking place in Connecticut just two months away in October, she invited me to take a trip to Miami to help her with wedding tasks that included lace cutting for the bridesmaid's dresses. In early August I flew to Miami with a guy I was dating. Though we had planned our stay for a week, I decided to extend my time to help her finish what we had started. The story of Pris and our connection to one another can only be due to God's plan, reflecting on how situations and relationships come to be in our lives. Sometimes, they are as invisible as where and how far the wind blows.

After my boyfriend left to fly back home, Pris informed me we would be joining her fiancé and his friend that evening who was going to be an usher in the wedding in Connecticut, so I would be meeting him regardless – even if I hadn't taken the trip to Miami. "Sounded great to me!" When they arrived to pick us up, she was in her room still getting ready. When I opened the front door, standing next to her fiancé, was this extremely attractive, suntanned friend with shiny blonde hair and bright blue eyes. Thirty-eight years later, Don Greenleaf is still, and always will be, my loving husband and partner for life. My knight in shining armor, my very best friend, champion, and angel sent from heaven! If you don't believe in love at first sight, just look at us and you will! The day after Pris and Robbie's wedding in October 1978, I took my leap of faith and tossed my own thread to the wind, as Don swept me off my feet and took me 1600 long miles away from all that I knew, down to Miami with him to meet his family. I was, at last, an adult, now uncontrolled and unimpeded to make my own choices and decisions, and free to express my own thoughts after enduring a tough, stressful childhood. We began our life together after I decisively broke away from my tangled, twisted, dysfunctional life in Connecticut.

I wrote a letter to the director of the theater in New York to inform him that I had moved to Miami and was handing over my part in the play before rehearsals were to begin in January. Don and I really were in love and compatible. I immediately found employment as the assistant to a purchasing agent for jet engine parts at Miami International Airport in order to do my part in contributing financially.

Five months later, in March 1979, he asked me to marry him and I said "Yes." Though I gave up my dream of becoming a Broadway singing star in order to spend the remainder of my life with the most amazing man on earth, multiple sclerosis would have surely stolen the show whatever my choice. However, the threads of my heart were far stronger.

On November 24, 1979, we paid for and put on our own beautiful wedding in the very church Don grew up going to with his family, and I was honored to become his wife – Mrs. Donald David Greenleaf. Louise Ann Huey Greenleaf. Now, Thirty-eight years later, Christ the King Evangelical Lutheran Church, is still our home. What a beautiful name, and such a gentle loving man that God has blessed me with.

Like the spider, we began to spin our own opus of LOVE, and I prayed that God would guide us along the way so when our earthly lives are complete, they will glisten to please Him for eternity, no matter what we face.

"Then make my joy complete by being like-minded, having the same love, being one in spirit and of one mind." -Philippians 2:2

Chapter 3

Stay with you

> *"I will stay with you when no one else is around. When the dark clouds arrive I will stay by your side."* ~John Legend

APRIL 1980

I am now five months married to the man of my dreams! My happily ever after! Our life is supposed to grow happier and more secure with each day, month, year, and decade! But now these feelings have returned *again* and are so much worse! We knew we had no choice other than to accept whatever this is called, but we needed answers so that we could learn how to deal with it, whether it will be temporary or long-term. We needed to stay strong, and focused together as partners.

After having spent almost the first two years of our marriage in doctors offices and test facilities – not to mention the small fortune we didn't even have, but had already spent on finding an answer – we demanded that an MRI (Magnetic Resonance Imaging) of my brain and spine be done, because after having spoken to people who had heard of these symptoms as a result of a relative, friend, or someone they knew who had the same similar symptoms, had been diagnosed with multiple sclerosis, and had also gone through the same stressful, muddy, dead end, road that I/we had also been dragged through.

When the MRI results came back, and we were called in to discuss the situation with the neurologist, he really didn't offer us a conclusive diagnosis. *"Well, yeah, it looks good. There's only one small lesion on the brain and two on the spine. Seems like the worst of this is behind you. You'll probably still have inflammation episodes – nothing a regimen of mild steroids won't relieve whenever one comes on. Just call me and we'll set you all up. No need to be uncomfortable. I think you're going to be fine in time."*

When I asked if it is called, multiple sclerosis, Don and I both remember the uncomfortable hesitation in his voice as he answered. *"Ah, could be, but for now, let's just call it neuritis, or inflammation of the inner ear, which seems to be the area that is triggering the symptoms."* Made sense to me! Who was I to question this expert? *"Hmmm, expert."*

In the spring of 1981, while still at the age of twenty-one, I had *finally* been diagnosed with multiple sclerosis – more commonly known as MS. It was after the diagnosis was confirmed; I realized my life would be changed forever, as MS makes sure to remind me *each and every moment of each and every day* that it is there. A person could allow it to take over and destroy their life, but for me, Amazing Grace! I mean, don't think at all that it's been some sort of pleasure ride. Far from it! Don and I were both devastated – me more so than him, as his strong faith since childhood kicked in right then and there as he rocked and held me tight while I cried like a child, for I had lost a precious treasure...my good health. And just as he assured me back when the symptoms started in the beginning of our relationship, again he promised that he will always love me and be there for me. Such a beautiful man I am so blessed to be loved by. Thank you, Don! Thank you, God!

MS is a chronic, progressive, incurable, and in many cases like mine, disabling disease of the central nervous system that specifically attacks the myelin sheath – a soft, fatty substance that acts as an insulated covering to nerve axons – like the rubbery covering around wires to electrical cords that are plugged into walls or other power sources. These axons are the body's wiring system which transmits electrical like impulses from the brain and spinal cord to the muscles, tendons, and nerves that empower *every* physical action in *all* living beings to occur. Such as the capability to walk, use our arms and hands; blink our eyes, and virtually *every* physical function that allows *all* creatures great and small, the power to operate. In other words, the myelin sheath in my body is literally like *Pac-dots* being gobbled up as they race through the maze of a *Pac-Man* game, as Pac-Man's endless greedy appetite continues to chomp away at the protective coating to the wiring system throughout my brain and spinal cord – short circuiting their ability to fully permit the conduction of nerve impulses that many of my major bodily functions are no longer able to perform normally. It is clinically called *demyelination*. This has created lesions or scars that have formed on my brain and spinal cord from the myelin that has been destroyed. I had later learned that MS is also known as *the disease of many scars*, and is also called *the snowflake disease*. Because, even though many of its beginning symptoms are experienced in numerous common ways, such as numbness, tingling, dizziness, equilibrium imbalance, optical disturbances, body fatigue (heaviness or lagging,) Its consequences by no means fit into a one-size-fits-all category. *Not one case is the same*. Because of the fact that the central nervous system is so highly complex, there has yet been a way for science to figure out exactly where it will target each individual, and how it will affect them. To me, it's like trying to predict *exactly* where lightning is going to strike during a storm.

After having already experienced almost two torturous years of being bombarded by all those crazy symptoms that were totally disrupting my life, such as constant numbness and sharp tingling in the fingertips on my right hand, as well as the toes on the right foot, intense pain from the knee down on the back calf on my right leg – as if it had been kicked or punched hard enough to leave a big, painful bruise, which hurts just as badly today as it did almost thirty-eight years ago. My gait, as I walked, was so completely and noticeably off-balance, that I felt extremely self-conscious about going *anywhere,* knowing that people were shaking their heads at me in judgment as they pathetically witnessed me walking crooked and running into things like walls, parked cars in parking lots, even falling as a result of tripping over my own two feet. With extreme embarrassment, I knew that I looked either drunk or on drugs, but there was *nothing* I could do to stop it!

I, then, experienced a six-week nonstop ride on the vertigo merry-go-round gone wild, which spun me so violently out of control that I couldn't eat or even keep a cup of water down. By the time vertigo had wreaked its havoc on me, my body weight had dangerously dropped from 105 pounds, down to 87 pounds. An alarming eighteen-pound plunge within just six weeks. Yes, I literally laid on my left side for all of that terrifying, agonizing time because it was the only position I could exist in stillness without throwing up even the bile from my already empty stomach. Just as soon as I would move my head in any other direction, the spinning immediately began with a vengeance. Try forcing yourself to stand up and walk with a saucepan in your hand to catch your puke, while at the same time steadying yourself with your other hand on every wall, grabbing every piece of furniture and countertop along the way. Think of what it would be like sitting down on the toilet and trying to keep yourself balanced as the room spins so vehemently out of control while simply trying to take care of mother nature without toppling off!

Shortly after getting the vertigo under control, I was then clobbered with an extremely painful condition in my right eye called, *optic neuritis* – inflammation of the optic nerve, which was accompanied with an annoying twitch just underneath the eye, causing me to be semi blind – as if a dismal screen or film had been placed over my eye – sort of like a dark window tinting. Like a shadow, I could see form, but no color or detailed features. I could see the light of something that blinked – like the flashing lights on an emergency vehicle, or a radio tower. But the light was dull and void of the brilliant brightness in its nucleus or center, and the dull light remained still – there was no blink.

My eye stayed in that state for what thankfully ended up being only about six years. Hey, it could've been forever, but one glorious Saturday morning – six years later, I felt an unexplainable change. A feeling of clarity. I asked Don to drive me to the blinking radio tower which was just a few miles from where we lived. As we approached the tower, and I closed my normal functioning left eye in order to see what would happen, WALLA! A miracle had been realized as I witnessed the brilliance in the twinkling of the tower lights. My vision had been fully restored! And even though this is surely a miraculous, feel good incident that God blessed me with big time, and one that I will *always* remember and be grateful for, still, I will never forget how I had to deal with all those crazy, frightening, and even some painful tests, that after all was said and done, turned out to be unnecessary, as I had been sent bouncing from doctor to doctor, who ran test after test, which *always* turned out to be NORMAL!

It was even more frustrating to know that I was raising the eyebrows on all of those important and highly recommended, highly educated and skilled physicians with the very best reputations – neurologists and ophthalmologists, who could not come up with even a clue as to what I was dealing with. Eventually their inability to give me a conclusive diagnosis had them stumped, so they started to question my mental stability, saying it was psychological, or that I was depressed. But my symptoms were REAL! Those horrid things that were happening to me were *not* made up in my mind like some crazy person seeking attention! It was infuriating to know that those doctors were dismissing my feelings! Every symptom I experienced pointed toward way too many of the classic onset indications of multiple sclerosis. I mean, c'mon, had they never in their careers encountered a case of MS, or heard of the high number of common symptoms that others had also experienced before they had been diagnosed? I was a newlywed, and for the first time in my life I was living in true happiness with the most amazing man, every woman dreams to name as her husband, lover, protector, provider…champion!

I'll never forget the stress and heartbreaking feelings that weighed so heavy on me as these awful incidences became more eventful and intense as our wedding day was approaching. I was even beginning to wonder if Don still wanted to marry me. But when he cupped my face with his hands and pulled his body into mine, he gently kissed me and told me he loved me, and that together as husband and wife, we would seek to find an answer.

So, we went on our way, and I began my first seven-week steroid regimen, which made me feel even better than my old self again. I believed it had done the job of *curing* me, even though I still had physical delays, like running, and my right leg dragging a bit – always feeling kind of heavy, and I still had that annoying screen over my right eye. Oh well, at least the dizziness was gone, plus I had gained my weight back. I was a strong, healthy young woman again. Praise God!

"And now these three remain: faith, hope and love. But the greatest of these is love." -
1 Corinthians 13:13

Chapter 4

Love of my Life

> *"From the moment I first saw you
> the second that you were born
> I knew that you were the love of my life
> quite simply, the love of my life."*
> ~ Carly Simon

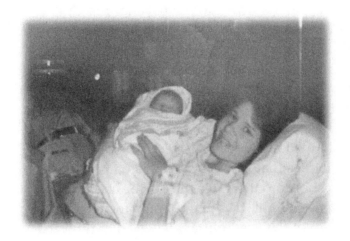

SUMMER 1982

Married life was surely moving along smoothly and happily, and thankfully, I had not experienced any more episodes since the diagnosis, and how good I felt even all these months after I had been off the steroid. Don and I were hoping to start a family soon, but we knew that we needed to discuss the matter with the neurologist. When he gave us the clear, we were filled with joy! Not only was he happy for us in that way, but also because I had been doing so well.

Whoever would have thought that dark and featureless figure behind the shaded lens over my eye was in reality a powerful, evil, and extremely cruel monster that had latched itself not only on to me physically, but even worse so, seeped its way into my psyche. Yes, little did we know that right before us, within the shadow of our bright and happy future, dwells an unwelcome entity that will continue to stalk my very essence, and seek to rob me/us of nothing less than *everything!*

In the fall of 1982, we were proud to announce that I was expecting a baby just a few short months after the doctor had given us the green light. I wore my pregnancy like a crown of flawless, glittery jewels that reflected a strong, healthy, happy, radiant woman. The wonderful part is that other than the eye issue – which still remained, there were *no* signs at all that I had experienced *any* of those horrible symptoms that had been tormenting me for so long. Both the entire pregnancy and the delivery were flawless. On Friday, July 8, 1983, I delivered a healthy six pound, eleven and a half-ounce, *perfect* and *precious* baby girl. In the instant her sweet little eyes met mine, together we saw God. Birthing a child into the world is truly the greatest miracle and gift that God gives. As I held her with a joy I had *never* felt before, that moment her tiny mouth found my breast, I was totally swept away as I felt the *forever* attachment of an unbreakable seal that would bind us together in love forever as mother and daughter. GLORY TO GOD!

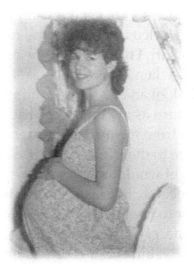

When she began to suckle, the realization hit me as to how dependent she is and *always* will be on more than *anyone else… Me!* I didn't want her to feel the anxiety that I was beginning to feel as I started to think about the what if's in a negative way. *"The MS, what if it returns? What if I'm holding her, and I suddenly become too weak or dizzy, or I go off balance and run into something, or fall with her in my arms? Oh my God, this is so unfair to her and to me for allowing these thoughts to invade our most sacred and crucial first moments together as mother and daughter! It will be okay, ALL of those crazy things*

I went through... They're gone... The doctor said so... God, please help me!"

In a flash, I felt this intense and indefinable peace absorbed throughout my entirety, accompanied by a sort of chaotic calm that continuously swirled around me and my newborn baby girl. I had felt this one other time in my life when I was seven years old, and in the blink of an eye, when I didn't know where else to turn as my innocence had been brutally taken from me in just a matter of a few moments – due to the frightening rage of one whom I thought would now always be there to love and protect me. But I was wrong, because when the door to my bedroom slammed shut, there I lay alone, crying and confused... beaten down physically, but worse so emotionally. *"Mommy, why are you letting him do this to me? God, please help me!"*

With my baby safely in my arms, and just as it had happened back when I was that helpless little seven-year-old girl, I again felt that immediate comforting presence of God, and discerned his loving advice. I didn't actually hear His voice speaking to me in words, but I knew exactly what the presence of His spirit was relaying to me.

Don't be afraid, Louise, I am here for you just as I have always been, and will continue to help you, Don and our wee baby girl get through this life together. Sometimes you will face some pretty bumpy roads with what will seem like endless twists and turns, but in the end you will think back and realize the untradeable joys that you have earned along the journey. And don't think for a moment that you'll be alone, because I'll always be right here in front of you, shining my light brightly along your path. You will also meet Angels along the way who will present themselves in different ways to accompany you and help guide you from steering off my path. Just always *remember my promise; do not let your heart be troubled, nor be afraid. It is peace that I will leave to you to go on and mother your child and gain wisdom in whatever you will face. Now go and run your very best race.*

Don and I chose *Kristen* to be her first name, and *Ruth* as her middle name, in honor and memory of Don's mom who passed away in April, 1978 – just four months before Don and I met in Miami. Though I, unfortunately, never got to meet Ruth, and neither would Kristen get to know her grandmother, still, I felt a powerful eminence of her aura around us. I know she was in awe and proud of this beautiful child her son, Don and I assisted God to create through our love.

Kristen Ruth Greenleaf (Krissy)
Friday, July 8, 1983
Thank you, God!

Chapter 5

Baby Mine

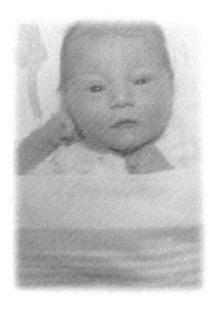

*"Rest your head close to my heart
never to part, baby of mine".*
~ Frank Churchill

It was such a joy when we brought our baby girl home to begin our life as a happy, loving family. I always knew that if I were blessed to have my own children, they would be loved and protected by me, their mother most especially, and with every fiber of my being they would have what every child deserves in that way. For there is nothing more comforting than the love of our mother, whether conceived in her womb or otherwise.

While I nursed her for the entire first year, I felt euphoric, both physically, and as my role as a loving wife and mother. *"I am here!" "I have arrived at the destination of my dreams!"* But within just days after weaning her from the breast, some of those symptoms started to return. I began to feel numb and heavy, stiff, and just a bit dizzy. *"Oh no, is the MS back? I have been doing so well, and the doctor even thought it was behind me. Please God, not now, I have my baby girl to raise!"*

I tried to ignore them, but I knew deep down that I might be in for some rough waters. It was as if that horrible shadow had been temporarily *overshadowed* by the miracle of how my hormones protected me during both my pregnancy and the past year that I had nursed. Now, it became clear to me that my sneaky stalker had been waiting patiently to strike at just the right time, when I thought that I was safe from any more MS attacks, and that I was now experiencing the joy that I had always longed to feel. Just when fear and panic started to overtake me, I felt that familiar, protective *'Peace which surpasses all understanding,'* as it says in Philippians 4:7 in the Holy Bible. Yes, it was God clothing me in armor, and equipping me with the necessary artillery that I will need to fight the battle of my life with Him and Don right at my back.

Thankfully, it seemed to just be a temporary adjustment of my body returning back to its pre-pregnancy state, and I was able to do everything that moms do to take care of their children, husband, and running and managing the home. Yes, I wore many hats, but I loved it! My dream had at last come true and I have my happy family now… Life is good!

Just around the time Krissy was three years old, I started to feel my right leg begin to drag again, along with an even more excruciating pain and tightness then I felt in the beginning. It wasn't allowing me a break, even in my sleep. I began to limp and drag my right foot, and could no longer trust myself to carry her while I walked. It was so hard for me to have to explain to her that she was getting too heavy for me to carry her. Neither one of us had been quite ready for the abrupt change, but it was necessary. At that point she really was getting too big for me to continue to walk and hold her at the same time. I'm just grateful that it's happening now and not when she was younger. I am especially grateful that I'm not dizzy and disoriented, and that I have no problem driving, and I am able to continue with my responsibilities. Limping and dragging had become my normal – ours together as a family. Hey, it is what it is, and you find your ways to make it work. One of the ways I find to help me get past serious bouts of anxiety, is to think back on beautiful memories.

Behold, children are a heritage from the Lord, the fruit of the womb a reward.
~ Psalm 127:3

Chapter 6

A Precious Memory

"Memory...is the diary that we all carry about with us." ~ Oscar Wilde

Sometimes, I can't help but to wonder just when it was that I took my *very last step*. I know it was sometime between 1989 and 1990, but I truly cannot remember the exact moment. However, I do hold a *most* precious memory in my mind that I love to revisit. It was the last walk that I took on the beach. Just me, by myself... no assistance. No cane, crutches, or wheelchair, just my own legs and bare feet, leisurely walking along the low tide water's edge on glorious Sanibel Beach – just as the morning sun had popped up to greet the day.

As I breathe in the delicious salty air, I enjoy the peaceful whines of seagulls hovering over the water, ready to swoop down and catch their morning meal. While I continue to walk, I noticed the countless number of seashells that washed onto the shore overnight. *"There so many!"* *I thought to myself. "I would love to start a collection, but I have no vessel to put them in. I'll just go back to the cabin and grab Krissy's beach pail."* But as I began to turn around, I felt that very familiar sensation of numbness, and sharp tingling in my feet, and heaviness in my right leg – like a weight holding it back and causing my right foot to drag in the sand. *"Hmmm,"* I wondered. *"More signs of the MS progressing? Oh dear, here we go again! I've been doing so well, but it seems to be happening more and more lately. Please, not now Lord, I have my little girl to raise! Looks like Cinderella's golden carriage is getting ready to turn back into a pumpkin... There goes my shell collection... So disappointing!"*

But then, God had a lesson for me. I felt His presence directing me to Look down and realize the treasure in one. One that is broken and imperfect, yet is beautiful and precious. I abided in the urgency to pick it up and carry it, and to keep it close – just as He carries me and keeps me in His close protection. Just as Krissy's mother, I keep her close and protect her always.

When I looked down at the sand, I noticed a small scallop shell lying right beside my numb and tingly foot. It had a hole near its center, and it was there, all by itself. I will always believe that God had placed it right there waiting just for me to pick it up. And so I did. As I observed it, I marveled at its beauty – even though it was broken and not perfect.
"You are just like me, little shell... Broken yet beautiful in God's eyes, and through the eyes of those who love me... My family, and friends. I'll keep you safe and visible always as a reminder each day when I look into the mirror, that I am a child of God. Broken, yet precious... valuable, though

flawed. And still, he carries us each as if we are all of the most brilliant quality and his highest priority. Funny how all the shells on the sand are marked with their own unique imperfections. Some more than others… Just like me, and you. The wonderful thing is that God loves us all unconditionally the same in his mighty and perfect way.

Yes, this precious memory of my last walk on the beach is one of my greatest gifts, and it is always just a thought away, just as his loving, protective embrace is always present as he carries me and my heavy load through it all. Through thick and thin, whether good or bad, happy or sad, glad or mad. And it makes no difference if I walk or roll, because he still sweeps me up and sprints with me safely in his arms. "I PRAISE YOU, LORD! I THANK YOU, LORD! I LOVE YOU, LORD!"

As I catch a glimpse of my beautiful broken shell, each morning when I roll to my table to brush my hair, I sing a little song to remind myself that God made us *all* in just the way that is perfect to HIM.

> "I consider it right, as long as I am in this earthly dwelling, to stir you up by way of reminder." - 2 Peter 1:13

My beautiful broken shell
I found on Sanibel
where the ocean meets the sky
your beauty caught my eye
so I picked you up
and will always hold you close
for you help me understand
We're ALL God's beautiful broken shells
along the sand

Chapter 7
Arms of Love

*Like a child who's held throughout a storm,
You keep me safe in your arms of love."
~ Gary Chapman, Michael W. Smith, Amy Grant*

As the years go by, my walking ability, along with the pain and heaviness continue to get worse. Just as Krissy's first grade school year began, we suddenly lost Don's sister, Jane, to a brain aneurysm. She was only 36 years old, and we were very close. She was my matron of honor in our wedding. I was so shocked and grieved by her loss – Don's entire family was of course, but the stress from it affected me to the point where I could hardly walk no matter how hard I tried. I conceded to using a cane, as I could no longer walk without assistance. I knew that the other moms and the teachers wondered about my limp but were afraid to ask, and I never felt like I needed to offer an explanation – though that would become necessary in the years ahead, as many of them were really *angels in waiting,* ready to come to the rescue when we needed them. So even though my limp was normal to Krissy, I was forced to explain my new addition to her and to everyone else. It was actually such a relief for me that I *finally* had a valid and visible explanation that something was physically wrong. Still, it would be sometime before I would say, *"multiple sclerosis."* Krissy understood as best as a six-year-old child could, I suppose – we just didn't make a big deal about it. No, Don and I were certainly concerned about my having MS, and the many changes that continued to come on out of nowhere, but we were against instilling fear in her and making her feel like we couldn't do this or that because mommy feels bad. Yes, mom had things going on, but we needed to keep life flowing at a calm and normal pace for all of us. And so we did, just as I continued to do most all of the things moms do. Even though I am a bit slower than the average bear and had to take more breaks, I wasn't going to miss out on the enjoyment I got out of volunteering at the school and at our church. Most of all, helping Don to raise Krissy. I refused to allow MS to take hold of me and disrupt our life!

I made sure to see my neurologist regularly, and though I would complain to him about newer symptoms, he never really saw them as any big threat or reason to be concerned. He would just write me another prescription for the prednisone steroid a few times a year, and then send me home. The stuff made me feel like Superwoman, and I was good to go for quite a few months before having to ask for more. He never refused when I requested a prescription, because he knew that I would resist for as long as I could before I got to the point when I had to, and I appreciated that he just wanted me to be as comfortable as possible. There wasn't much they knew about MS – or so I was told, except for the fact that inflammation plays a large part in where in the body it attacks. It seemed to be like a foreign, mysterious illness that the doctors had no clue what to do with, or how to fix, however, the anti-inflammatory drug called prednisone proved to be the most effective drug to offer relief. But I had *never* been informed and was ignorant to the fact that it was depleting the strength in my bone density, which proved that some day's possibility, would become *today's* reality of *osteoporosis.*

Less than a year after I started using the cane, I needed more upright stability, as the cane was causing me to lean forward and making my back sore. I was also hunched over and looked like an elderly person. Believe me, I like elderly people very much, but at this point, I'm only thirty years old! So I purchased a pair of crutches and started walking with just one. It didn't bother me at all because I could sling a bag over my shoulder to carry things in while still holding Krissy's hand as we walked. But just as importantly, Don and I could also continue walking hand-in-hand together. It is my favorite way to be in my life – close and in hand with my two greatest loves.

It was the saddest and deepest pain that I had ever felt when the separation occurred because of having to go to both crutches. Even writing this now makes me cry as if it had just happened yesterday. It wasn't so terribly bad with my seven-year-old though, as walking independently is much more welcome than having to hold mom's hand all the time. I got over it quickly though because it's a natural transition that is supposed to happen as our kids get older. Isn't teaching them independence a goal we labor to help them reach? Isn't independence a privilege we *all* strive to keep? That *wasn't* what I wanted to hear though when Don and I could no longer walk hand-in-hand as we *always* had. *Always* like two happy lovebirds that were seen by all as *inseparable* and *inspirational*. How blessed I am especially, to have such a gentle loving man as my husband and father to our child.

On **August 24, 1992** – which was to be the first day of Krissy's fourth grade school year, Miami was hit with one of the most devastating hurricanes in United States history. Hurricane Andrew's fury did a hellacious job of destroying miles, upon miles and miles of *everything* that was in its path – including our home, our church, our neighborhood, Don's business offices! Hardly anything throughout a vast number of miles was recognizable. Most roads were inaccessible due to the countless fallen trees, bushes, foliage, and strewn objects that were blocking them. Electrical poles – wooden, as well as concrete, were all snapped in half with live wires tangled and dangling within the countless fallen trees and on the ground. Power was out everywhere!

Because we live only about a mile west of the bay water – which flows into the ocean, our area was highly encouraged to evacuate in case of storm surge and flooding. Since Don was born and raised here in Miami – his childhood home, where his eldest sister still lives, is located around fifteen miles inland, so we gathered all of our important papers – insurance policies, checkbooks, cash, and our dog, and we stayed the night and weathered the storm there.

When the barometric pressure in the atmosphere dropped as the storm neared landfall, my body suddenly went completely limp from the waist down. It was so frightening to have zero control of myself and not even be able to stand with the assistance of my crutches! Anytime throughout the night when I needed to use the restroom, Don had to literally lift me on and off the toilet. It sure was a long, scary, sleepless, and *very* stressful night, as we had no choice other than to listen to the sustained high winds outside whipping around ferociously, while heavy rain pelted the house in all directions. Severe lightning flashed as thunder continuously boomed loudly throughout the night. When the electricity suddenly went out, we knew it was because the huge, oak tree in the front yard that had stood so majestically in its spot since long before Don's three older siblings even came along, as well as an enormous cactus that was located just outside to the right of the front door had fallen. It was a wonder and miracle that Krissy slept through the worse of the storm without a stir!

When Andrew finally passed and morning came, I was so grateful that my body returned back to its normal state and I could walk with my crutches again. We opened the front door to assess what had taken place all night while the four of us were thankfully safely huddled on the hallway floor with blankets and pillows. The sky yielded a smoldering gray and sinister appearance – like a raging fire had been extinguished. We were all shocked and saddened at the site of the giant oak that was uprooted and knocked to the ground – covering most of the front yard, along with the tall, thick, spiny cactus that was downed and destroyed by the storm's monstrous fury as well. As we scanned the entire neighborhood to see that so many large, old trees had fallen with their branches and limbs scattered in *every* direction, Don and I realized that since the hurricane has caused this much of a mess this many miles inland, and farther to the north of where the eye was projected to hit further south, closer to where we live, that we needed to leave to get back home sooner rather than later.

The drive home was sad and chilling! What normally would only be a twenty-minute drive from Joanna's house to ours, took closer to three hours as we witnessed the devastating destruction. It was as if bombs hit in every direction visible. Roofs were torn off homes, businesses, restaurants – etc. Windows were blown out of *every* structure we passed, and some were even leveled to the ground. The tall, thin pointed steeple with a cross at the top of the Baptist church – just a few miles northwest of our house was snapped off from the high winds, leaving a giant hole where the rain no doubt left the inside in ruins. We begged the Lord that lives were not lost in this monstrous storm!

Since Don had no other choice, he was forced to very carefully navigate and detour through people's muddy front yards that had already been deeply trenched by the tires of other vehicles also trying to find their way home. Essentially *every* road leading to our house was blocked by fallen trees and scattered debris. We dreadfully realized that the farther south and closer to our home we got, the more destruction we saw.

When we *finally* rounded the corner of our street, we were smacked with the reality that our neighborhood was also severely trashed. It brought painful tears to all of our eyes when we saw that the back of the William's house - three doors down to the west of ours, was leveled to the ground - no longer there! We hoped and prayed with everything we had that they were *not* there, but were safe somewhere else. As we pulled up to our house, we couldn't help but notice that Tom and Mary's carport across the street was mangled and contorted into some really crazy shapes - as was our basketball hoop that stood between our driveway and the grassed edge of the side yard.

Turning into the driveway, our house looked as if it fared very well compared to most of the others on the street. Don had Krissy and I stay in the car so he could take a look inside and around the property to make sure everything was safe for us. But of course, that's Don, *always* thinking of us and our safety first.

"What's taking him so long?" we anxiously and impatiently questioned. But when he returned, the look on his face, and that rare but familiar sad tone in his voice, quickly clued me in on the reality that he did *not* have good news for us. *"I'm going to drive the car to the front entrance and have you come in through the front door,"* Don said. *"Krissy, honey, I need you to be strong and help me guide mommy through the house because the floors and carpets are wet, so the rubber bottoms on the crutches will not grip the tile floor to hold her up. The house is in bad shape and it's going to be hard to take in. We're going to be shocked and cry, but thank God, we're all alive and safe, and We WILL get through this together."*

It wasn't as bad as I was expecting when we first walked through the front door that leads straight into the family room on the south side of the house. None of the windows were broken – not even the double sliding glass doors in the family room and kitchen that lead out to the pool patio and backyard. However, it was so heartbreaking to see Krissy having to realize that the screened enclosure around our pool patio had collapsed. She and I both gasped at the sight of the large pieces of its dark gray metal supports that were bent up, twisted, and scattered all along the brick pavers. Some of the screens were even still attached, flapping in the wind.

Debris was all around and inside the swimming pool, and the water was filthy black. I sensed her thinking back to Friday afternoon when she and all of her neighborhood friends were here for a pool party to belatedly celebrate her July eighth birthday while they splashed around and played games in the sparkling blue water.

The tile floors were all wet and slippery, and the carpeting in the sunken living room was completely saturated. "But why? I wondered. The family room, as well as the dining room and kitchen, were intact just the way we left them before we evacuated. *"I'm so sorry about our enclosure and the trees that are down and covering the entire back yard,* "I said to Don. *"But the rest of the house fared well!" We can put up a new screen enclosure as soon as we get the pool all cleaned up again,"*

"Louise, Krissy," he said in a dispirited tone again. *"The storm came in from the East, which is the side where our bedrooms and hall bathroom are. All of those windows were completely blown in – that's where all the water has come from. Large pieces of glass and countless shards are completely covering the beds, head pillows, and carpets, and ALL of our stuff in EVERY room is blown around like a cyclone hit!"*

While holding onto one another, we carefully stepped through each room to check out the damages. It was a heart-wrenching experience for all three of us, to say the least, as we sobbed at the shocking magnitude of the storms vandalizing effects, as well as the innumerable possessions that were either heavily damaged or destroyed.

When we got to Krissy's room, our poor nine-year old was grief-stricken beyond any way she had ever displayed. Her cries were agonizing. This will surely go down as a pivotal experience she will *never* forget! All the gifts she received from her party, Friday were on her bed – soaked and destroyed! The numerous ribbons that were displayed along the wall top she so proudly won competing in horse shows hung crooked, buckled and damp. Her large collection of stuffed toys she carefully propped up after making her bed every morning was wet as well. But the saving grace we were so blessed to celebrate, was when she noticed one of her small stuffed bears that were tossed by the wind, had landed perfectly lodged and stuck between the double closet doors where much of her belongings were stored, including her clothes, shoes, photo albums, dozens of videos. Most valuable to her though – the beautiful red and white wooden barn Don built for her to store her prize equine horse collection was ALL spared from being damaged – thanks to that little bear blocking the doors from being blown open.

After we got through the initial shock from the damage inside, we then ventured outside where we were relieved to see that most of our neighbors were safe and accounted for – even though *every* house on our street and throughout many miles all around us suffered extensive damage – some much more than others. We were informed that the Williams up the street who lost the back of their house, were still on vacation out of state. Unfortunately, there was no way to contact them or even our own relatives, as electricity was out everywhere. It was just too dangerous to go outside the neighborhood. Even with my crutches, it was extremely hard for Don to keep his eyes on both Krissy and me when we were out, so as soon as we could, we purchased my first wheelchair to use on longer walking excursions when away from home. In three years' time, I went from limping to using a cane, to one crutch, to two – then ultimately to a wheelchair by the time I was only thirty-three years old with a nine-year old child to bring up.

    The entire experience was traumatizing, and it surely was a tough and trying year rebuilding our homes and community. But with God's loving presence we all got through it. Talk about a lesson in patience! Talk about realizing our strength when faced with any of that which is beyond our control, especially since we were given only a few hours to prepare our homes, gather supplies and seek safety, as Andrew very rapidly intensified into a ferocious category five hurricane. And even though it forced me to buy a wheelchair, I mostly walked with my crutches. Thank you, God, for keeping us safe through the storm in your comforting arms of love.

"God is our refuge and strength, an ever-present help in trouble." -Psalm 46:1

Chapter 8

Angels watching over me

> *"All night, all day, Angels watching over me, my Lord."* ~ Otis L. McCoy

Angels – they seem to appear out of nowhere and just when you find yourself in situations when you need them the most. There have even been times I've wondered if perhaps *I* was the angel who came to the rescue of another. Countless incidences have occurred in my life where getting out of some sticky situations would have been impossible on my own without the help from some form of divine intervention. So, being the Christian woman that I am, although you don't have to be a Christian, or a member of *any* monotheistic religion for that matter, to believe this, I know that *Angels do exist!*

I have been able to count on angels to come to my rescue before I was even born. It's as if God knew of the struggles I would face throughout my life and assigned angels to rescue me at the drop of a hat, as I have experienced so many random, unusual, unexplainable, and nearly unbelievable things that happened to me as far back as I can remember. This was most evident during those years when darkness, loneliness and depression invaded my life and stripped the joy from my spirit, as though great efforts were made by some cruel and evil force. I'm especially happy and thankful that the worst of those days are over now, or perhaps I have learned to roll with the punches in a more tolerant and accepting way, as sorrow and sadness will inevitably continue to come. Not only for me, but for *you*, too, as well as for *every person* that dwells on this planet. The reality is that *no one* is exempt from facing hardship and sometimes even danger. But then again, it is how we choose to respond when experiencing dark times that leads us to the miracle of an intercessory angel. That's when I am certain and have no doubt that I have *Angels watching over me!* Yes, and not just for me but they are there for *everyone*, and when we allow ourselves to be aware of their presence, that is when we are able to realize how we were miraculously lifted up or led away from a threatening or dangerous situation that we could most assuredly *not* have been able to wriggle out of on our own.

However, not everyone believes in angels, and some may have no problem telling you that they think you're a little odd to say that you do. Well, I'm here to tell you that *I surely do believe*, there have been far too many encounters throughout my life for me not to realize that it was my Angels who pulled me away from possible harm or jeopardy. Anyone who knows me would agree that I could *not* have been able to take care myself on my own without assistance and there was no other person present that could help me. Though there are countless occasions that I can tell you about, I would like to touch on one incident in particular.

FEBRUARY 1995

It was hard to admit to everyone, even to myself, that I had been slowing down again. My legs and feet were in agonizing pain, waking me up from my sleep in the middle of most nights! My reflexes were becoming more delayed than usual. Uh-oh, I thought, what is happening? It was even beginning to show up in my driving. My foot would miss the pedals sometimes. But stubborn and in denial, I kept telling myself that I was still doing well – that it had only happened a couple of times – everything would be just fine!

One afternoon when I was backed into a space in the school parking lot, waiting for the bell to ring and for Krissy to come out, a bus filled with a baseball team from another school pulled up and parked in front of, and across from, the spot where I was parked. I should have had no problem clearing it when it was time to leave. Once the driver stopped and turned off the engine, some boys in their baseball uniforms came out and stood in front of the bus, just across from where I was parked. They stood around for a few minutes, laughing and high-fiving one another then carried their equipment to the playing field.

Right at that time my daughter came out to the car. School had let out for the day and it was time to go home. When I started the car and put it into drive, I couldn't quite make it around the bus, so I shifted into reverse and started to back up. As I did, my foot slipped off the brake pedal! It felt swollen, heavy, and numb. And my reflexes were not quick enough for my foot to press the pedal so that I could ease the car back just far enough to reposition my wheels in order to clear the bus. Instead, I smashed into the car that was parked next to me when I lost control of my foot. Krissy cried out, *"Mommy, what are you doing?"*

Now, here's where Angels swooped down to lead us into safety in this particular event.

Thankfully, we were both all right, but I knew that I had caused some damage. Thank goodness no one was in or near the car that I had hit. I waited for about a half an hour, but no one came out to the car. One of the moms who witnessed the crash helped me write my name and phone number on a note for the car owner, because I had become shaky and nervous from what had just happened, as the MS had already started to affect my hands. I hadn't told my husband or anyone else what I had been noticing, as I myself was in denial of what the disease was doing to my body. She was truly an angel for keeping me calm and helping me with something so simple, yet something I had trouble accomplishing on my own.

We left the information on the windshield and went home. The lady who called was a substitute teacher at the school that day. When she reached me, she was so nice and rather surprised that I had left my name and telephone number for her to contact. I had to; I damaged something that belonged to someone else… her car! I would never have left without making sure my contact information was in a secure location on her windshield and easy for her to see. Most importantly, I had to show Krissy the proper way to handle such a situation. I needed to teach her the right thing to do. You don't just leave because no one is around to see, but you take responsibility for your mistakes and choices, and how we show others as well as ourselves that we can be trusted. It's what gives us inner peace, even when we may have to pay a price. Life is *not* always easy!

The cost of the damage ended up being around $250.00, not a terribly high price to pay, but it could have been. I had a hard time sleeping that night, remembering those young boys who were standing at the bus... laughing and full of life. What if they had still been standing there and I was going forward instead of in reverse when my foot slipped off the petal? How would I have avoided hitting them? Or what if someone had been crushed while walking between the two vehicles – what if? How would I have been able to live with myself for the rest of my life *knowing* that my physical abilities were progressively diminishing, just to hold on to the ability to be able to jump in the car and come and go as I please? The scenarios were endless, and I couldn't continue to beat myself up over these what-ifs. Hey, no one wants to give up their independence, certainly not me, but I realized at that very moment that it was becoming a danger for me to continue to be behind the wheel and driving on busy and often dangerous roads. The time had come that I had to stop driving altogether. I could have hurt or killed someone – those boys, or an innocent person walking between the cars, myself or my precious daughter... NO!

It was a choice I, thankfully, made on my own and *not* because I was forced to, as I have no doubt that God's angels are *always* around the bend and on the watch to help protect me physically, as well as when it's necessary for me to make sound decisions.

When we arrived home from school and I told Don what happened and, also, about the difficulties I had recently been experiencing, together we made the decision that it was time for me to turn in my keys. Lovingly and responsibly, we both agreed that it was the proper and necessary thing to do, and that he would take over the task of getting Krissy wherever she needed to be without any interruption to her being a normal and happy kid. This did not mean that our lives would come to a screeching halt – on the contrary! When good friends, members from our church, and moms from the school heard about our situation, these multitudes of Angels came to our rescue and made sure that Krissy would be picked up and brought home from school each day. When Don arrived home from work, the three of us as a family would go to the stables where she rode her horse after school and after completing her homework.

We continued to carry on as a happy, loving, and grateful family. On Sunday mornings we attended church with our wonderful congregation filled with saints and angels – all helping one another and others throughout our neighboring community, as well as people who struggled in places far away in need of help from God and His heavenly angels.

> *"For he will command his angels concerning you to guard you in all your ways." ~ Psalm 91:11*

Chapter 9

Jesus take the Wheel

> *"Jesus take the wheel*
> *Cause I can't do this on my own*
> *I'm letting go*
> *Save me from this road I'm on*
> *Jesus take the wheel"*
> ~ Hillary Lee Lindsey / Brett James / Gordon Francis Sampson

I thought when I was forced to buy my first wheelchair after the hurricane three years ago, even just to use when we went places that required a lot of walking was devastating, but giving up my total independence at 36 years old was even harder. How will we manage? Don already had more than enough on his plate. He was now going to have to take on ALL of the driving responsibilities, such as getting our daughter to and from school, as well as to her activities, AND at the same time, run his business and now work even harder than he already does to pay our way in life. An even greater load is now all on his shoulders! We are not going to cave in to this! We will find our way! We will stay strong and keep our faith that God's presence will guide us through.

People were wonderful and so helpful. Friends and neighbors helped me to run necessary errands, while other parents helped by getting Krissy to school and her activities while Don was at work. It worked out nicely for the first few months, but I was frequently asking the same people to make room in their own very busy lives. They were even starting to make it clear that it was getting old, and many times now, they would come up with reasons as to why they could not help. Even though I certainly understood, still I knew that the time had come when I had to not ask so much. Don't get me wrong, people were still there for sure, just not as often as I needed. There's nothing that will knock your confidence and self-esteem down more then the feeling of realizing you have become an annoying little bug that won't stop pestering. I felt so little, so UN!

    Look, It's hard to be such a young woman, wife and mother abruptly stopped by no doing of my own, to carry on with the everyday necessary chores and running around tasks that I truly took great pride in and loved doing – like the grocery shopping, doctor appointments, gas for the car, the dry cleaners, and the endless list that goes on and on. These things don't stop having to be done, so we hired a woman from our church to drive me around once a week for four hours at $10.00 an hour. It was $160.00 to $200.00 a month that we had no choice but to add on to our monthly budget Don very diligently managed even before he and I met. He was raised to work hard and to be a good provider for himself and one day a wife and family.

While I continued struggling to keep up the pace of normal everyday living. I found myself becoming weaker and slower when trying to accomplish simple tasks that should just happen automatically. My muscles were so tight, stiff and in pain all the time, and as I said earlier, whenever Don would try to massage my legs to soothe and stretch them, they would kick out from going into full spasm, causing the right one especially, to stiffen up so rigid, it was like trying to bend a 2 x 4 piece of wood.

MARCH 1996

Krissy is now in the eighth grade at this point and still had a few years to go before she would be of age to get her driver's license. I needed to find some relief, quick, as it was very obvious that the every-other day subcutaneous injections I had been taking for the past three years, was doing nothing to slow down the progression of the MS as we hoped it would have by now. These new symptoms, or exacerbations, were no longer only lasting for short periods, but they would come on more intense, as well as remain permanent. Am I rapidly advancing beyond the point of no return?

Multiple sclerosis is a disease that progresses in stages. It normally starts out at a level called the **Relapsing-Remitting** stage, which is how most cases are triggered for whatever reason, and apparently is how mine began to show its signs back in the spring of 1979 – just two months before my 20th birthday, and eight months before our wedding. Disturbing symptoms such as what I described in earlier chapters would just come on me out of nowhere! They would bother me for a time, and then just disappeared. Then, as soon as I recovered and thought the worst was gone – BOOM, on came something new, lessening my capabilities even further. Well, even right from the onset there were some things that have to this day never come back fully – like that area on the back of my right leg that has never stopped feeling like a big bruise, and the burning, tingling, and numbness, especially in my feet and hands. There are a couple of major things – like the loss of sight for six years in my right eye that I am ecstatically grateful have not reappeared. But, I do not ever take it for granted that just because that has not befallen again on me for the past thirty-two years, does by no means guarantee that it cannot nor will not happen again. In reality, I am inclined to believe when looking back from the very beginning, that my MS in all probability, stayed in its relapsing remitting stage for only about a year before it transitioned into the **Primary Progressive** level, which is when newer symptoms remain permanent. No more breaks…the party's over! What awaits me/us in the future?

We were so optimistic and hopeful when the first subcutaneous injecting interferon drug became approved to slow down, or perhaps even halt the progression in patients with Relapsing and Remitting multiple sclerosis in 1993. But because of the high number of people with the disease throughout the country, anxious to get on something that would give relief, for about the first year, the drug would be available only to those whose names were drawn through a lottery system, because of short supply for the hundreds and thousands of' desperate people with MS seeking to get on it. Though my name was one that was chosen, I thought it would be best to wait for a year and see how it was affecting others. Maybe that sounds a bit selfish or cynical, but looking back, it would not have made a difference regardless, as I was already thirteen years diagnosed into the disease – fifteen really, from the very first symptoms in 1979, and had unknowingly long passed the relapsing and remitting stage. In all actuality, it had never even been explained to me that there were different stages, and there was no Internet available to do my own in-depth research. I just trusted that the doctor knew all the answers.

> *In their hearts humans plan their course,*
> *but the Lord establishes their steps.*
> *~ Proverbs 16:9*

Chapter 10

Changes

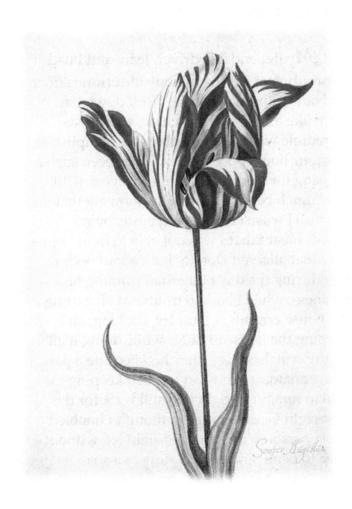

> *"Ch-ch-ch-ch-changes*
> *Turn around and face the strange.*
> *I watch the ripples change their size*
> *But never leave the stream"*
> *~ David Bowie*

MARCH 1997

*M*y dependable driver, Jean, and I had our routine of getting my outside errands done and out-of-the-way for the week down pat. We were like a well-oiled machine, and it was incredible what we were able to accomplish in just four hours once a week. It has been such a blessing for Don and me this past year with how much better I felt inside, knowing that just because I wasn't driving anymore, by no means meant that I was not able to figure out a way that allowed Don to think about nothing else during the day other than running his business, while I had no trouble at all getting the house errands, – laundry, cooking, and keeping the house in order while doing it all on my crutches. Hey, they had become a part of my anatomy, and had assisted keeping me able to remain upright and still walk for the past eight years. And even though I hobbled like a person with a pegged right leg without a knee to bend, and moved slow as a snail, I didn't care one bit how comical I must have been to observe, because they allowed me the freedom to get where I wanted to be on my own, and in my own time. I pray that my legs will always remain strong enough to use them, because it really bothers me so much when I have to be pushed around in the wheelchair. The good thing about it, though, is that it saves time and makes getting me around so much easier for Don and Jean.

What a blessing it was to still be able to walk with my crutches for most other things, like being picked up by a friend and meeting at a nearby restaurant or someone's home to have lunch with a group of girlfriends from church. Another friend picked me up every other week to have our fingernails done together, and another every single Friday in order to attend Bible study. But most importantly, I could still go to the church and help out in the office folding the bulletins for Sunday services, answering phones, and a list of many other necessary tasks that required the help from volunteers. Yes, we were a large group of women between the ages of mid-twenties to mid-eighties, who were bonded together as we met quite regularly as a sisterhood in service of our Lord, Jesus Christ, our congregation, and others in need around our community.

I was involved in several ministries, both on my own, and, of course, as a family with Don and Krissy. I sang with our magnificent choir as an alto and a soloist. Don and I were leaders for our large youth group and organized and chaperoned trips for the kids and helped with service projects. We enjoyed being guides and good influence to the young people, and delighted in watching them grow in their faith journeys, and Krissy loved that we were there to spend these special times together. Don was an usher, counsel member, and the head of our buildings and grounds commission, and Krissy sang with the youth choir and attended Sunday school. We were a family who wholeheartedly attended church service each week, committed to serving in the ways in which we were called.

My most fulfilling was an organization that a small group of women from our church started back in 1989 – most appropriately named, "Love in Action." LIA is a not-for-profit ministry that takes care of not only the necessary basic needs for 23 foster care families around our area – consisting of approximately one hundred and fifty children from birth to 18 years of age. The ministry grew into a sizable network of women who heeded to the call of pouring out their genuine love to these innocent children who had been abandoned, neglected, abused, or all of these unconscionable acts that were committed by the very ones who brought them into this world. By no fault of their own, they were placed into these strange homes, where most of the time they were abruptly taken away from their situation to be cared for with six to ten other kids they did not even know, but were in their same situations. They were literally ALL court authoritatively removed from the custody of abusive, drug addicted or jailed parents. These innocent children had no other family and nowhere else to go, and so many were sadly born addicted to and affected by hard drugs that their birthmothers used throughout their pregnancies. A number of them had siblings who they were separated from depending on their ages, and available space in each home.

One of my favorite events was assembling age-appropriate Easter baskets for the Easter Bunny to hand out to each child during our annual Easter party we put on for them every year. It was awesome to see the magic in their eyes and the smiles on their faces when they received their baskets. It sure was a lot of work putting them together, but so well worth the time and fulfillment we were blessed to feel. When we chose the date to assemble the baskets at our planning meeting, I volunteered to bring lunch for all of us when we were finished with the baskets.

I got up a little earlier than I normally do that morning to make a big platter of assorted sandwiches and packed chips and beverages to go along with our lunch. I felt great and had plenty of time to read the newspaper before I showered and got myself ready to go. It was always so important for me to shower, put my makeup on, and do my hair before I began each day. Good grooming had always been a very important part of being me. Presenting myself clean and well-groomed was something I was taught from my auntie Sue at a very early age. I didn't wear expensive clothing or use expensive makeup, but I did always make sure to present myself as one who very much cared about my appearance. That's a good thing!

"Do you not know that your bodies are temples of the Holy Spirit, who is in you, whom you have received from God? You are not your own; you were bought at a price. Therefore, honor God with your bodies". ~ 1 Corinthians 6:19-20.

When my lovely friend, Milre, who was one of the original masterminds behind the constructing and launching of this amazing ministry picked me up and drove us to the church, we immediately went to work filling baskets with Easter grass in all colors of the rainbow, as well as filling plastic eggs with jellybeans. We, then, placed a number of age appropriate goodies, such as, a small stuffed toy for the infants and toddlers. Each child's basket included a fun age appropriate goodie, such as Easter themed coloring books and crayons, a small box of marshmallow peeps, a book on the story of Easter. The older boys may have received a deck of cards, and the girls a scented bottle of lotion, along with a Bible, and everyone except for the infants received a chocolate Easter bunny. It was a lot of work, but great fun, and it filled our hearts with joy.

After our lunch break, something strange was coming over me. I felt dizzy and sort of feverish! In minutes, I became so disoriented that I could hardly function! Milre gathered all my things and drove me home. After she left, I immediately got on the couch, pulled open the recliner and fell asleep. Don came home a while later to say hello and check in on me as he did most days. I told him that I was not feeling well, but was comfortable relaxing on the couch. He still had to go back to work, but I told him that I was cold and asked if he would put a blanket over me before he left. He did that, as well as set the portable phone next to me in case I needed to call him. Then, he kissed my forehead and went back to work. Krissy had track and field practice after school, so I was not worried if I were to oversleep.

Don was not gone very long when I woke back up having to use the restroom. When I went to get up, my body was stiff as a board and I had no strength in my legs to push the recliner down. I started to release all over myself, and the couch – good thing it's leather! I needed to get up, but I was so weak. I didn't even have a cold or anything. I was really concerned with the way I was feeling and that I needed to get cleaned up! I scooted to the seat next to me and somehow pulled myself up. It took what seemed forever to make my way to the bathroom. I don't know how, but I managed to get myself into the shower and rinse myself. I knew I needed to get out of there quickly though, as I was getting weaker by the second. I barely dried off, but was able to put my long nightshirt on and pull it down. I knew that I needed help, and as I started hobbling back to the couch, when I got to the front door – which was about halfway, something told me to unlock it. I did and was able to finally get back to the couch. I thankfully was able to think to bring the towel I used to dry off with to the couch to throw it over the mess I had made. I was so disoriented by now that all I could think of was Milre's phone number. Not Don's Beeper or Mrs. Fisher next-door. It was Milre's number that came to my mind. I pushed the buttons real slow and careful. When she answered, I said, "please, I need help – the front door is open."

The next thing I knew, paramedics were standing over me, and Milre was patting my forehead with a wet cloth. Don had been notified and was pulling into the driveway. Through all of this, I was even able to give them Dr. H, my neurologist's number. He told them to get me to the hospital. I didn't want to go in the ambulance, so they helped Don put me into his truck. I was stiff as a board. Neither I nor anyone else could bend me at all. My body limbs were completely spastic. Sort of like a dead body that rigor mortis had already set into. It was like trying to force a manikin into a seated position.

When we arrived at the hospital, Dr. H. had already instructed them not to give me any medication since I was not in life-threatening danger. He wanted to see if my body would go back to normal on its own. It took about two hours. I asked him if I had done something to cause such a severe attack, and why did I even have it with being on the interferon injection for four years now? He said that I did nothing to cause this attack. For some reason, it just came out of nowhere. I wasn't overdoing or stressed – It just happened. Don and I were concerned that perhaps this injectable was not doing its job. At almost $1000 a month, $10,000 a year – you get two months free – what a bargain! Thankfully I had good health insurance that covered the ridiculous high cost, but at the same time, I felt guilty and my heart ached for those who could not afford insurance so that they too could have the possibility of feeling relief from this treacherous disease. Life can be so cruelly unfair!

After my body had completely relaxed and it was time to go home, Dr. H. wrote me out a prescription for an antispasmodic drug that came out in the early 1970s to relieve spinal cord injury, cerebral palsy, and patients who endure severe spasticity. Spasticity is a condition which often occurs as a consequence followed by brain trauma – which would be defined as a severe blow to the head from either a blunt strike, or disease. Spinal cord trauma happens when the actual cord has either been severed or has become severely inflamed as a result, more than likely, from a fall or contact injury. Tragically and sadly, the results can incur paralyzing and permanent effects on the victim – specifically the whole or partial loss of sensation and movement in parts of the body – arms, legs, or both, with a high percentage having to live the remainder of their lives confined to a wheelchair, and so many having to become totally dependent on others for EVERYTHING!

Spasticity also inflicts it's rather annoying and painful effects, such as tight stiff muscles and uncontrollable spontaneous twitches that are beyond pain I cannot even begin to define! Think of it as a rubber band stretched to its limits and twisted so tight that if you made one more twist, it would snap! You wish for relief – for that band to be unwound just a few times so it would stop feeling as if you were tied down on some torturous medieval stretching machine. It accompanies various diseases that affect the central nervous system – epilepsy, cerebral palsy, stroke, hypertonia – which is abnormally increased muscle tone and loss of flexibility. And in my case – multiple sclerosis.

This oral anti-spasmodic drug that was prescribed to me was essential and offered welcome relief in just a matter of days. Within a week after starting the drug, it was like a miracle! The spasms and tightness lessened dramatically and I had more flexibility than I could remember having since before this crazy journey began. The problem that arose though, was that as the drug accumulated and absorbed through my entire system – my brain and organs, I became so extremely relaxed to the point of almost a zombie like being. I had a family to take care of! Children came over to our house after school to play in the pool with Krissy, and I was the responsible mom in charge. I was so unsound and unfocused. What in the world am I doing? How do we continue on like this? I cannot give up! I will not surrender! With the help of God, I WILL find a way! PLEASE LORD, I AM AFRAID, AND I NEED YOUR HELP!

But I didn't feel as if God was hearing my desperate cries as I continued to exist like an incorporeal being, hardly able to function as the drug continued to cause undesirable side effects such as chronic fatigue, weakness in motor skills, depression. All of these symptoms affected me in these ways, and now I was depending on using the wheelchair everywhere I went except in the house where I used my crutches. I felt uncomfortable around everyone, even my closest friends. People were always asking me questions, and I never minded answering their inquisitive wonders about multiple sclerosis and their desires to learn about it, but the inquiries became so personal – even from strangers. It seemed every person I came across made sure to take a little more than a peek at me, then quickly moved their eyes away when we made eye contact with one another. But I always made sure to offer them a bright, sincere smile, inviting them to smile back. Many times they did, but even more so they turned away as if I were invisible. It came to the point where I just wanted to be left alone, and I wanted people to stop asking questions. I wanted to just hide from the world! Again, I felt so UN and so little compared to everyone else. Yes, I lost precious treasure – I lost me, I lost God. I needed Him and I kept calling, but He didn't come. I tell you, I don't know how I was able to hold it together for my family. Don and Krissy were both so understanding and patient, but we were losing me and I couldn't find her. That person who always kept that bright smile and had kind words for everyone. I always made sure of that for Krissy, especially. It's what I longed for all of my life – just for people to be kind back to me.

Don was left with no choice other than to find ways to juggle everything in his oh so busy schedule – along with checking on me several times throughout his work days. Because having been on the drug for all these months now had pretty much kept me slow and lethargic. I was experiencing chronic fatigue, weakness, clumsiness, diminishment in my motor skills, and merciless depression, which both physically and emotionally assaulted most of my days – especially when I was home alone. I cried over EVERY little thing! I was only thirty-eight years old and my libido was pretty much shut down. Don and I had ALWAYS enjoyed our frequent private times together, but that part of me as I said, was pretty much shut down. Though he never once complained about holding it all together, still, I sensed that deep down he carried a heavy sadness for the situation we were in. I did too, and I made sure to give my time to him when I had the energy. It was heart wrenching and frustrating at the same time for him having to watch me, his love, suffer in the state I was in, and having to wonder if he would be left without his wife, and our daughter left without her mother. He is the truest meaning of love is patient and love is kind. Will our life be like this forever now? GOD, PLEASE HELP US!

> *"It is God who arms me with strength, and makes my way perfect." ~ Psalm 18:32*

Chapter 11

Don

> "Cause no, I can't deny
> This love I have inside
> And I'll give it all to you
> My love, my love, my endless love."
> ~ Lionel Richie

My husband, my love, my very best friend,
the father of our sweet daughter, Krissy.
You are the glue that holds us together,
the rock that keeps us solid,
the MOST selfless person I know.
How and why do I deserve you?
You are gentle and kind, softhearted,
yet firm when necessary.
You are fair, yet strong in your convictions.
God truly blessed us all with you.
But more than anyone, God blessed ME the most
when we were joined together to share our lives
as lifelong, loving, partners in marriage.
And it did start out just that way too.
We worked and loved so well together.
For us and to make sure that
Krissy
had the life we only dreamed of when we were kids,
That's okay though, cause we both made it through
didn't we?

And then,
MEAN, NASTY, VICIOUS, MULTIPLE
SCLEROSIS
crept in on us and robbed us
of our beautiful partnership together.
ROBBED YOU, DON!

Robbed Krissy of watching us
be what loving parents should be together,
of all of us working and playing together as a
fun, loving family.
But this isn't about MS today and woe is me.
this is about YOU, Don.

Please always know how much I love you
and appreciate ALL that you are to me, Boo,
and the world you function in.
You give of yourself ALWAYS when you can.
you give of yourself FULLY when needed.
You are SO special!
Much more than you will ever admit to.
But don't worry, babe,
I'm not the only one who sees
THE MAN, THE HUSBAND, THE FATHER,
and the LOVING, GIVING person that I know
and get to share every day with.
All those who know you do too.
Yes, honey, truly we do.

I WILL LOVE YOU FOR ALL OF MY DAYS.
And if my days are to end and we must part.

Cry for me just a little – for us.
Please don't ever forget the me who you fell in love with.
Please don't ever forget the beautiful love we shared together.
But PLEASE pick yourself up, let us go, and go on to enjoy the rest of your days.
Find someone who is sweet, pretty, HEALTHY, self-sufficient.
Someone who will always accept that Krissy
And her family MUST and ALWAYS
Will be a very big part of your life.
Make sure she is someone who will be there for you,
The way you were ALWAYS there for me.
THANK YOU FOR THAT, MY LOVE!

And thank you for working so hard to be
The BEST provider for our daughter and me.
I LOVE YOU, I LOVE YOU, I LOVE YOU!
ALWAYS AND FOREVER, my love.
My endless love!

~Me~

Chapter 12

This is my fight song

> *"This is my fight song*
> *Take back my life song*
> *Prove I'm all right song*
> *My power's turned on*
> *Starting right now I'll be strong*
> *And I don't really care if nobody else*
> *believes*
> *'Cause I've still got a lot of fight left in me"*
> *~ David Bassett / Rachel Platten*

LATE FALL 1997

I have been existing like a soulless corpse now for the past eight months – unable to keep from dozing off during even just a simple conversation. I was aware of it, but the drug was so strong, there was nothing I could do to stop it from taking me over. This must be what it is like for those who are trapped in a physical affliction, fully knowing what is being said but unable to verbally communicate in order to express THEIR OWN desires and opinions. How sadly frustrating!

Then, early one evening, while I was in the bedroom getting ready for an event Don and I would be attending at church – it's the only place I would go now. He came running into the bedroom, turned on the TV and said, *"You have to watch what's coming on after the commercial!"* When the reporter returned and began his story, I watched and heard in amazement. He was talking specifically about *"spasticity,"* and people with conditions I spoke of earlier – cerebral palsy, spinal cord injury, epilepsy, brain injury. He also mentioned, *multiple sclerosis.*

"New reports are out that they have been able to liquefy an anti-spasmodic, muscle relaxing drug, (the exact same one I had been taking!) *and send it directly to the spine through an implanted, computer programmable device – referred to as an intrathecal infusion pump. The device is surgically implanted in the patient's abdomen, with an attached catheter that is fed through the intrathecal. (the canal within the spine containing cerebrospinal fluid) The medication is then released continually throughout the day and night from the reservoir, which is just about as thick and as round as a hockey puck, to a catheter which sends the medication directly to the spine, eliminating the debilitating side effects experienced by those who ingest the drug orally. Patients are receiving great relief from this new break through. Some patients are even regaining full motor skills and walking ability. For further information, call the number on the screen."* Don and I both knew right then, that this was something I needed to look into. God has always guided me toward the right direction, and steered me away from bogus cures and treatments.

When I called the number, I was informed that there was going to be a seminar in regards to this new procedure. One of the nation's well known top neurologists and experts on multiple sclerosis, and was also the one who developed the procedure, would also be the speaker. A good friend from church drove me up and we had a lovely and informational day. She and I were both impressed with what the doctor had to share. I brought the information home to Don, and he was also impressed. *"This could give me my life back. No, it's not a cure, but it is a relief, and maybe, just maybe I'll walk again, drive again, be free of the pain that I have had to endure for so many many years. What a treasure it would be to feel back to normal again! A treasurer I lost so long ago. Maybe I have found it again! Maybe my smile can be truly joyful again! Maybe my husband and I can have a completely normal intimate life together again! Maybe Krissy and I can go to the park and walk, and play in ways like we were not able to when she was little. Maybe through me, people with these illnesses will see that there is hope. That hope can become reality. That you don't have to give up, and wither away. That faith in God and prayer IS REAL!"*

EARLY JANUARY 1998

With much excitement, I brought Dr. H. the pamphlets I had brought home about the new breakthrough and procedure. I was disappointed and rather surprised though, that he had no idea this was even out there and approved, but it surely did stir his interest. He told us he wanted to research it and find out more before moving forward with such a delicate procedure. He said it made perfect sense though, and promised that he would get back with us as soon as he found out more about it and what all it entails. Don and I so appreciated both his honesty and his interest. When he was finished with my exam, he wrote me out a new prescription for the oral medication. He said it was necessary that I continue taking it in order to keep my severe spasticity under control. Though I was not happy knowing I would have to go on existing like a zombie, as I had for the past ten months, Dr. H. assured us that he would get right on to learning about this, and would get back with us as soon as he was comfortable. He told us that it would take some time, but not to worry. If it is possible for me to benefit from this, we *will* make it happen.

MAY 1998

On May nineteenth, two days before my thirty-ninth birthday, Dr. H. called with the good news we had been waiting for. *"Congratulations, everything is a go to move forward with the pump." We have you scheduled to be admitted into the hospital for an outpatient procedure in July. At that time, we will do a lumbar puncture in order to administer a small amount of the drug into the base of your spine. If your body reacts positively to where the spasticity is lessened, we can go ahead with the pump procedure after everything is set and scheduled with a neurosurgeon."*

JULY 1998

Within 30 minutes after the lumbar puncture and administration of the drug on that July morning, my legs and toes felt wonderfully free from tightness and pain. I was able to feel sensation and wiggle my toes Oh, it felt SO good!

On Wednesday morning **OCTOBER 21, 1998** – one year and seven months after hearing about this miracle of modern technology – specifically for the very condition I suffered with for so many grueling years, my pump was placed into a pocket on the right side of my abdomen that was created by the highly skilled hands of my neurosurgeon, Dr. GA. It was a bit hard having both abdominal and back surgery at the same time, but a very small price to pay for what I prayed for and hoped was soon to come.

We knew we were going to need help during my feeble two-week recovery period, so we had a keyless entry pad installed on the outside wall of our garage door. Through Milre's love and incredible organizing skills, she signed up around thirty women from church, who lovingly took turns coming over and took such kind, gentle care of me on a daily rotating schedule during the hours Don and Krissy were at work and school. The keyless pad was a godsend as each was given the code in order to open and close the garage door as they came and went.

Because the doctor ordered me to lay flat in bed until the excruciating headache brought on from the movement of the cerebral fluid during the placement of the catheter had past, I was not able to do *anything* for myself – not even get up to go the toilet. And of course, I needed to allow the small incision on the lowest of my back to heal, as well as the area in front where my now protruding Titanium Angel rests inside of the pocket Dr. GA created on the right side of my abdomen. It is located about an inch and a half to the right of my navel, and looks almost like an actual hockey puck. I thought it appropriate to name it that because it is made of titanium...a durable metal that is actually stronger than steel, yet lighter in weight. Titanium is nonpoisonous and corrosion resistant, which gives it the ability to serve in many different ways, from aircraft parts to jewelry, and even as an ingredient for some cosmetics. What makes it particularly unique, is that it is nonthreatening to the human body and is able to be used safely as medical devices both inside and outside of the body, bringing great hope and relief to people who suffer in different ways. It is used to make prosthetic limbs, bone replacements, and such as in my case, devices that are used as reservoirs in order to store liquid medications that are used to deliver and relieve chronic illnesses and conditions continually around the clock. It is located about an inch and a half to the right of my navel, and now it lives within me. I am blessed.

My warmhearted angels from church literally fed me with their hands while I was laying down. They put the bedpan under me and cleaned me. They brushed my teeth for me, and sponge bathed me. They did our laundry, kept the house tidy and vacuumed, and while one was here at the house with me, another was at the grocery store shopping for us. Don didn't have to worry about putting a meal together for over two weeks. My beautiful nurse friend, Jeane, stopped by on her way home from work every other day to clean and change my dressings. As the intensity of the headache began to fade, she brought over an old pair of shorts and a T-shirt, and actually got in the shower with me and scrubbed me good with soap, and washed and blow-dried my hair. My head was clearing from both the headache and being off of the oral drug. It felt SO good that I was starting to feel back to my old spunky self again. My favorite was when she rubbed my body with a lovely scented lotion. When I looked in the mirror, my eyes sparkled, and I smiled at myself with joy. I was proud that with the help of God, I made this happen. Having my life back was in my reach. Mine, Don's, and Krissy's.

I am so thankful to my kind, caring, friends for loving me and my family so much that they did all that for us. I will ALWAYS be grateful to ALL who kept me, Don and Krissy in their prayers, sent cards, flowers, meals, gifts and phone calls. I hold Milre especially dear in my heart for putting this all together. Love surely is the *greatest* treasure I have been blessed to receive.

I am living proof that these devices will be hugely beneficial to many who suffer with severe spasticity. For me it was immediate relief once the proper dosage was set by Dr. H. turning his computer on as he simply scanned a mouse over my new pump. He then set his programmer on a dosage number he could only guesstimate might be comfortable, and I was the one who could make that determination. If the dosage was set too high, I would be too weak and flaccid – like I was when I was taking the oral pill. If it was too low, I was stiff and tight – like I was before the pump was put in. It took a few appointments before we were able to find my perfect comfort zone, but when we did, it was incredible! Within three hours of the adjustment, my pain was gone! I started sleeping like a baby! No more fatigue, my bladder became completely normal again, and Don and I were back to enjoying the physical side of our love again, just the way God meant it to be! I WAS BACK! *Glory Hallelujah! Praise and thanks to God!*

    I went to physical therapy for seven months, three days a week. Once again, my angelic brigade took turns getting me to and from. We purchased an adult three wheeled bicycle that I rode around the neighborhood for enjoyment, to stop and talk to neighbors whom I had not been able to interact with since I started the oral medication, and to further strengthen not only my legs, but also my cardiovascular health as well. As each day, week and month went by and I became stronger and stronger, the reality set in that I would probably *not* walk on my own again without my crutches. But that was okay with me, because the physical therapy retrained my pelvic area to where I was standing with perfect center of gravity and equilibrium, and walking very well with my crutches. I knew it was time for me to get back on with living independently again. I am much too young and have more energy than I know what to do with to be stranded.

Since I realized for certain that my feet would not be able to work the gas and break peddles on the car, I decided I wanted to have hand controls installed. My AWESOME love man bought me a brand new, Toyota Solara and had the controls installed for me.

In **JULY 1999,** Krissy turned sixteen, got her driver's license, and I started taking hand control driving lessons with a physical therapist...Miss Hamburger... who specialized in teaching the handicapped to drive with them. I loved driving with my hands and arms even more than the usual way with gas peddles and brakes. I always loved driving! Three months later in **OCTOBER 1999,** I not only got my driving privileges back, but my life! I am blessed and grateful! We passed my old car onto Krissy, and now, together, we have both unfurled our wings of freedom.

When the school year began in the fall, she entered her junior year. It was such a relief for Don not to have to do so much running around, and I felt fantastic that I was back to doing my chores and volunteering and wherever I chose to go. The world was my oyster! I'm here to tell you as the saying goes, *"You don't know what you've got till its gone"* is SO true! I packed the wheelchair in the trunk, slid my crutches along the floor in the back of the car, and had no problem asking for help from anyone. There was always a wonderful someone eager to help. I am blessed!

In late **MAY 2001**, our baby girl graduated from high-school, then went onto college at a university five hours north of our home. The time had come to let go so she could become further educated and wise in the ways to become self-sufficient. With the help of God, I have no doubt that Don and I, did our very best as her parents teaching her to become ready for this very moment.

It was actually easier than I thought it would be because we would drive up to visit her every six weeks or so, and she would come home during holiday and semester breaks. The times in between were quite nice for Don and I as we had entered into our second half of marriage, and rediscovered our partnership together as husband and wife again.

In the **winter of 2003,** I became quite ill from a flu that had hit me and then kept me in the wheelchair permanently. I could no longer stand or even take a step. My crutches were no longer a part of me. Though I was no longer able to walk – even with the crutches – I still had a large network of friends who were willing to pick me up and maneuver the wheelchair in and out of the trunk. Plus, I was still strong enough to stand up at the car door to help me in and out, and then they would wheel me wherever we had gone – whether it be the church, to a restaurant to meet all the other ladies for lunch, one of their homes, doctor appointments, or wherever. Gosh, I will ALWAYS remember the loving kindness of so many true friends and angels sent from heaven. Especially, Susie Lindstrum, Chris Summers, Donna Hennessy, Cindy Falkey, Sue Grigg, Celia Huertez, Janine Armstrong, Cindy Rosasco, Sandra Reed, Milre Pedersen, Doris Peterson, Cathy Sockwell, Peg Brewer, Ginny Fogel, Dr. Amy Mulmsberry Kaye, Jen Diego, Ana Mancado, Jeane Adams, Petra Rodzewicz, Virginia Nugent, Susan Lewis, Pastor Kathryn Carroll, Sharon Williams, Pat Horner, Luz Hanson, Lucy Martinez. Janet Fisher, Kitty Finneran, Eileen Armeao, Elaine Melgard,

Adelle Schwabe, Emily MacElfresh. If there are names I neglected to mention, please know that my gratefulness is no less for you then the above names.

Krissy graduated from college in **DECEMBER 2004.** Then, just two months later in **FEBRUARY 2005,** she became engaged to her college sweetheart, who was in the R.O.T.C. program with the United States Marine Corp. Don and I, of course, gave them our blessing. Then, right after he graduated in **APRIL 2005,** he received his orders to report to basic training in Quantico, Virginia. Wow, suddenly I was faced to realize that the five-hour car drive from our home to the University was no big deal at all, as we could just hop in the car and go to see her – or she could drive home as often as we wished. But, now, a fourteen hour, one-thousand-mile drive would no longer allow us the option to see her as often. The reality suddenly set in that our little girl was now an engaged woman, ready to begin her own journey with the man she chose as her life partner.

When Don finished helping them pack up the moving truck, we embraced and said our final, tearful goodbyes, we got in our car and slowly drove away, waving until we were out of view of each other. It felt as if the umbilical cord made its final detachment. I was experiencing so many mixed emotions going on at the same time. Happiness and excitement for her and her fiancé, and for Don and I as well. But also, sadness and wonderment of what life is going to be like for Don and me without her close by? I pray we've prepared her well.

They chose New Year's Eve, December 31, 2005, for their wedding date, here in Miami, at the the very church she was baptized, she and her daddy were both confirmed as kids, and he and I were married. Now, I am the mother of the bride! My daughter! How awesome is that? I have a wedding to plan!

OCTOBER 12, 2005

About noon, as I was heading west on S.W. 112th Street and 77th Avenue while driving home from running errands, I had to stop for a red light at what is normally a very busy intersection. I even thought to myself that it was very unusual – especially for this time of day -- that there were no vehicles stopped at the light across from me heading East or passing in any of the other directions. As I waited patiently, I joyfully sang along to Elton John's, *Crocodile Rock*. When my light turned green and I proceeded to drive, suddenly, I was T-boned by a vehicle that came out of nowhere from the South direction. They ran their red light and sent me spinning all the way across the intersection. When my car stopped spinning and came to a stop, I was then heading East. I did have my handicap placard hanging on the rearview mirror. They tell you not to have it hanging while driving, but it never impaired my vision in any way, and I always thought that if anything were to ever happen it would at least let someone know that I am disabled.

Of course, I was shaken and frightened after the car stopped, and my left arm, which worked the gas and break lever was sore. But at the moment of impact, and while the car was spinning, I felt an incredible calm come over me. Just the same as that which came over me right after Krissy was born. Just like the assurance I felt when I was a little girl with no choice and was in fear of my safety. And, just like countless times throughout my entire life…especially with this crazy disease when I felt God was right there with me.
In a matter of moments, a beautiful woman with long, dark hair knocked on my window. She was wearing scrubs and directed me to turn the window down. But, I could not move my arm far enough to reach the control, so, she opened the door and asked if I was alright. I

told her that my arm felt a little sore but I knew it wasn't broken or damaged. It just felt like I had been punched. My main concern was when I asked her if anyone was hurt? She said, "everyone in the other car was fine." She asked me, "What is your disability?", and I told her, "Multiple sclerosis." She said, "oh, my goodness," "I am a Beta Nurse." That is a nurse who comes to the home of someone specifically with multiple sclerosis, in order to instruct the newly diagnosed how to administer our daily injections, and offer us tips on how to lessen the side effects of the drug. I was astounded, and so was she! She called the paramedics, and also tried calling Don, but could not reach him. At that time, I started crying. First because I did not feel it was necessary to go to the hospital, secondly my car was smashed up and thirdly, because I was just downright scared!

Now, another woman and her daughter came to the passenger side of the car, and the woman asked if she could come and sit in the passenger seat to help calm my nerves. I said, "yes." Her name was Patricia, and she was also wonderful. She told me that she was a counselor for handicapped children in the public school system. Wow, first the Beta Nurse, and now the counselor for the handicapped. She and her daughter also said that they witnessed the crash as they were walking home from the Yom Kippur service at the Jewish Temple down the Street. The person who hit me ran their red light and crashed into me. I couldn't believe all the people from the Temple who had witness the crash as they were walking from the Jewish Temple. While I was stopped at the red light, I saw nobody! But, in reality, there were many. Who else could it be but Jesus, sending angels to help keep me calm and safe until help arrived? Then, the Beta Nurse answered and spoke to Don. He told her he was on his way. I was so happy and relieved to know he would be there soon.

In the meantime, the paramedics arrived and two young, very muscular men exited, then immediately came over to my car. The one who was the driver saw my handicapped tag and asked if I was able to walk. I told him no – that my wheelchair was in the trunk. The other man took the car keys out of the ignition and opened the trunk to get my chair. Then, it was the driver who gently lifted me out of the car while the other man rolled the chair over to us. Then the driver lowered me into my chair. I thanked them both for helping me – especially the driver guy who lifted me. He told me that it was his pleasure. He told me he helped take care of his grandma who was in a wheelchair for many years before she passed away, and that's why he loves doing what he does. That brought tears to my eyes.

By now, Don had arrived and I felt so much better. The police also arrived and was writing the report out with the person who hit me. I was so happy no one was hurt.

Though our car was crushed up pretty good – probably totaled, I felt fine, and told Don and the paramedics it wasn't necessary to take me to the hospital. After they checked my arm and vital signs and cleared me, Don took me home. It was on that day, **WEDNESDAY OCTOBER 12, 2005**, less than three months before Krissy's wedding, I drove for the last time I ever will again in my life. It could have been so much worse though if the accident happened before all of the wedding tasks on my part were done. So, I am surely thankful that it went off without a hitch.

AUGUST 2017

It has been 19 years since pump number one was put in. At this time, I am on number four, as each must be replaced surgically, approximately every six years or so before the battery expires. If that were to happen it could be a very dangerous, or even fatal occurrence. I had a serious emergency situation pop up back in 2007, and care not to ever have to go through that horror again. The normal protocol is to replace the pump only, and for the surgeon to simply reattach the existing catheter during the procedure. Therefore, he merely reopens the original incision, detaches the catheter, removes the existing worn out device, then, simply places the new one back into the original pocket, reattaches the catheter, sutures it up and you are good to go for another six or so years. The nice thing is that the recovery period is to simply allow the incision to heal. I must go to my neurologist's office every three to four months so they can refill the medication. This is another very interesting procedure in itself. Without going into detail, it is like going to the gas station to fill your tank back up – only mine is the medication – liquid gold to me and the others who are lucky enough to have one. The invention is ingenious and helps many people to live better quality lives, as well as helping our caregivers to move us around so much easier.

Because a cure for multiple sclerosis has yet to be discovered, it remains progressive and incurable. Though the pump has certainly been a godsend in helping Don and others to move me around easier for all of these twenty-three years, still, the disease continues to keep me uncomfortable in so many other ways. Even the pump no longer helps with my spasticity nearly the way it did. But, I cannot complain. I have been blessed and I am grateful beyond words that I was able to enjoy the prime years of my life with the comfort I would not have known without my titanium Angels.

As I sit in my wheelchair and watch the trees sway, hear the birds sing, and delight in watching butterflies fluttering around my beautiful front and back yards through my windows, I reflect back on this journey with a strengthened spirit. Through these long and trying years, I am most grateful that God, my father, in Heaven, has *always* been and will continue to be right here for me – just as he promised since I was that confused little seven-year-old girl. Hey, who knows what lies ahead when we are so young and life moves us forward during both joyful and difficult times. But because of His unconditional love for me and each and every one on this earth, God whispers in our ears, gives us the choice to find faith and strength to travel on His lighted path where we learn, give thanks and find the joy in our journeys no matter what we face.

Now here I am on my own. I am sitting at the top of an unfamiliar, steep hill with my training wheels removed. The time has come to make my choice to release the brakes. Do I have the courage to face what's before me unscathed? Or, will I crash and fall apart?

Oh, oh! I hear the sound of thunder beginning to rumble. The sky is darkening, and it's beginning to rain. A storm's coming from the east. The trees are dancing in the wind. I have no other choice now but to ride the storm so I can get back home. Please, God, keep me safe! I choose to keep rolling. No matter how many times I get punched, I WILL keep getting back up!

"Ask and it will be given to you; seek and you will find; knock and the door will be opened to you."
~ Matthew 7:8

Millions of Reasons to Smile Today

As we waken this morning
let us mindfully pray,
for some millions of reasons
to smile today.

An abundant buffet
clad from heaven above,
overflowing and bursting
with God's holy love.

For each leaf on each tree
may all count as one.
Every bird that flies by,
and the warmth of the sun.

To each whom we meet
let us greet with a smile.
Take a peek at the clouds,
even just for a while.

Vision strawberries, butterflies, prayers,
children laughing;
rainbows, puppies, and flowers in bloom.
Poetry, music, elderly wisdom,
a stroll in the park in the cool afternoon.

All wondrous gifts
like the coo of a dove,
just as everyone smile
is the laced with God's love.

Then when the day ends
let our memories portray,
ALL those millions of reasons
we smiled today.

July 14, 2017 Monday

AN ENDING NOTE

Hello my friend!

    The sun is shining bright this morning, and some of my orchids are in full bloom smiling away at me. My nurse has already been here to get me bathed, fed, my muscles massaged, exercised, and laundry done. Wow, now I have a few hours to turn on beautiful music as I journal words that God gives me to share. I LOVE starting my week off like this! I LOVE that I am blessed with time to enjoy and appreciate the simplest things when I look outside and delight in the quiet, nonstop goings-on right here in my own front and backyards. I hope you'll get to take some time to marvel at something simple and free today, and remember it as you fall asleep tonight. Let it make you smile and give you peace and assurance that not everything comes with a price, and that there are countless gifts for us to encounter and savor every single day, even if just for a moment. The wonderful thing is that you get to store these things in your memory bank and enjoy them over and over again. It's like the scent of a fragrant flower. No matter how long you breathe into it, the scent remains just as sweet and aromatic.

I believe we are all aware that it seems more and more evident our lives have become beyond busy these days. We are jam-packed with endless responsibilities, and exorbitant activities, that we are losing touch with taking even just a snippet of time to relax our minds, and nourish our souls with the simple and abundant gifts that are *everywhere* around us. I pray you, too, will gather some priceless treasures to tuck away in your mind to enjoy today and every day.

Thank you for taking the time to read PART ONE of ROLLING WITH THE PUNCHES ~ My Persevering Battle with Multiple Sclerosis. I pray you will continue to walk beside me while I continue on pushing my wheels in PART TWO.

God bless!

Louise Huey Greenleaf

---If you would like to contact Louise Huey Greenleaf, you can email her directly at lgsprout@aol.com or visit her on Facebook. She would love to hear YOUR story. ---

Rolling With the Punches is available on Amazon Worldwide and also available for download on Kindle.

About the Author

Louise Huey Greenleaf has dauntlessly survived the ravaging effects of multiple sclerosis since her symptoms began in 1979. Despite her confinement to a wheelchair and battling through the emotional ups and downs of living physically challenged, Louise decided to exercise her love of writing by sharing her profoundly overt words in order to invite awareness and instill compassion – not only to those with multiple sclerosis, but to the numerous chronic illnesses that affect the lives of countless men, women, and children throughout the world, here within the pages of her *solo debut book* – **Rolling with the Punches ~ My Persevering Battle with Multiple Sclerosis.**

Louise is an award-winning author and poet. Her works are included in seven multi-author compilation contest books with Spiritual Writers Network/Transcendent Publishing. She is also a contributing author in two books with OptiMystic Press, and the world renowned author, inspirational speaker, spiritual teacher and psychic medium, *Sunny Dawn Johnston*.

Louise has also been an inspirational, keynote speaker to groups around her community, addressing the subject of living positive despite her physical challenges.

"She believed she could, so she did."
-R. S. Grey

Rolling with the Punches

Rolling with the Punches

Made in the USA
Middletown, DE
22 June 2025